ULTIMATE
FOOTBALL HEROES

TRIPPIER

FROM THE PLAYGROUND
TO THE PITCH

DINO

Published by Dino Books,
an imprint of John Blake Publishing,
2.25, The Plaza,
535 Kings Road,
Chelsea Harbour,
London SW10 0SZ

www.johnblakepublishing.co.uk

www.facebook.com/johnblakebooks ⬛
twitter.com/jblakebooks ⬛

First published in paperback in 2018

ISBN: 978 1 78946 050 6

British Library Cataloguing-in-Publication Data:

A catalogue record for this book is available from the British Library.

Design by www.envydesign.co.uk

Printed and bound in Great Britain by Clays Ltd, Elcograf S.p.A.

1 3 5 7 9 10 8 6 4 2

Papers used by John Blake Publishing are natural, recyclable products made from wood
grown in sustainable forests. The manufacturing processes conform to the environmental
regulations of the country of origin.

Every reasonable effort has been made to trace copyright-holders of material reproduced in
this book, but if any have been inadvertently overlooked the publishers would be glad to
hear from them.

John Blake Publishing is an imprint of Bonnier Books UK
www.bonnierbooks.co.uk

For all readers,
young and old(er)

ULTIMATE
FOOTBALL HEROES

Matt Oldfield is an accomplished writer and the editor-in-chief
of football review site *Of Pitch & Page*. Tom Oldfield is a freelance
sports writer and the author of biographies on Cristiano Ronaldo,
Arsène Wenger and Rafael Nadal.

Cover illustration by Dan Leydon.
To learn more about Dan visit danleydon.com
To purchase his artwork visit etsy.com/shop/footynews
Or just follow him on Twitter @danleydon

TABLE OF CONTENTS

CHAPTER 1

ENGLAND'S FREE-KICK KING

Luzhniki Stadium, Moscow, 11 July 2018

With the sound of 78,000 football fans ringing in their ears, the England players walked out onto the pitch in Russia. Their captain and top scorer Harry Kane led the way, followed by their super saver Jordan Pickford, their big centre-back Harry Maguire, and then Kieran.

It was hard to believe what was happening. Three years earlier, Kieran had been relegated from the Premier League with Burnley. Six years earlier, he had left his childhood club Manchester City to challenge himself in the Championship. Now, at the age of twenty-seven, he was an England hero and he was about to play in a World Cup semi-final.

'Come on, Kieran!' voices shouted from the crowd.

The whole Trippier family was there supporting Kieran in Moscow: his dad Chris – England's biggest fan – his mum Eleanor, and his three brothers, Chris Jr, Curtis and Kelvin. Without them, Kieran could never have made his football dreams come true. And next to them stood his beautiful wife Charlotte and their amazing son, Jacob. Kieran was desperate to win the World Cup, for them and for the whole nation.

Gareth Southgate's inexperienced England team was making the country proud again. They had beaten Tunisia, Panama, Colombia and Sweden. Now, only Croatia stood between the Three Lions and the World Cup final. Whatever the result, it would go down as England's most successful tournament since the summer of 1990, before Kieran was even born! After years of disappointment, the fans finally had something to cheer about:

'It's coming home, it's coming home,
It's coming, FOOTBALL'S COMING HOME!'

As the English national anthem played in the stadium, Kieran sang along loudly with his teammates. Many of them felt like family to him. He set up goals for Harry Kane and Dele Alli week in, week out at Tottenham, and he had known Kyle Walker since the age of seventeen.

For most of those ten years, Kieran and Kyle had battled each other to be the best right-back around – in the England youth teams, and then at Spurs. At last, however, they were playing together in the same team – Kyle in the back three, and Kieran as the wing-back.

'Are you ready, Walks?'

'Yeah, let's do this, Tripps!'

Southgate's tactics were working brilliantly, especially for Kieran. This would only be his twelfth international cap but he was loving life with the Three Lions on his shirt. So far, he had been one of England's star performers. His incredible crosses had set up goals against Tunisia and Panama, and he had also scored from the spot in the penalty shoot-out against Colombia. What could Kieran do now in the semi-final against Croatia?

In the fifth minute, Dele dribbled towards goal but he was fouled by Luka Modrić. *Free kick!*

It was in a good position for shooting, but who would take it – Kieran or Ashley Young? They had both been practising and they both stood over the ball, waiting for the referee's whistle. So, who was feeling more confident about scoring?

'I've got it, Youngie!' Kieran decided. He was fearless and he had a good feeling about this one. He was in the best form of his career.

At Tottenham, it was Christian Eriksen who took the free kicks, but Kieran wasn't called 'The Bury Beckham' for nothing. This was his chance to show off his perfect technique on the world stage, just like he used to do at Manchester City, Barnsley and Burnley. All those years of practice had led to this one big moment. He was ready.

Kieran ran up and curled the ball over the wall and into the top corner. He made it look so easy. 1–0!

Goooooooooooaaaaaaaaaallllllllllllllllllllll!!!!!!!!!!!!

Kieran felt like his chest was about to burst with pride and joy. The World Cup semi-final – what a time to get his first-ever England goal! He slid across the grass on his knees, with his arms out wide as if to say, 'Look what I've just done'. Scoring for his country was simply the best feeling ever.

'Tripps, you legend!' Harry cried out as he jumped on his teammate.

'I'm still taking the next one!' Ashley laughed.

Soon, Kieran was at the bottom of a big team bundle. Thanks to him, England were winning. They were on their way to the World Cup final!

But after a mind-blowing few moments, he managed to calm himself down. There were still eighty-five minutes left, and England had plenty of work to do. Just like in their first game against Tunisia, they had chances to score a second goal but instead, they conceded one. In the second half, Croatia crossed from the right and Ivan Perišić beat Kyle to the ball. 1–1!

'Heads up, keep going!' Harry shouted out to his tired teammates.

Did the England players have any energy left for extra time? Kieran did his best to move forward and create more chances. He curled a corner-kick to John but his header was cleared off the goal line.

'So close!' Kieran groaned, putting his hands on his head.

He chased back to defend but by then, every single step hurt. They had played five tough games of football in only twenty-three days, and Kieran's body was telling him to stop. Soon, it was all over. Perišić flicked the ball on and Mario Mandžukić pounced. *2–1 to Croatia!*

As the ball hit the back of the net, Kieran's shoulders slumped. He couldn't carry on. Four minutes later, he hobbled off the pitch with the help of two physios. It was a sad way to end his wonderful first World Cup, but the England fans clapped and cheered for their exhausted and tearful hero.

'We love you, Tripps!'

After the final whistle, Kieran returned to the pitch to thank the fans for their support. As he stood there beside Southgate and his teammates, he felt the pain of losing but also an enormous amount of pride. Against the odds, they had achieved so much together.

No, England weren't bringing the World Cup trophy home, but they had brought football home. The excitement was back, and so was the passion. They had seen it in the crazy videos on social media, and they could feel it right there in the stadium.

'Bring on Euro 2020!' Kieran thought to himself.

Nevertheless Russia 2018 was a tournament that he would never ever forget. He had been fantastic, from start to finish. With his incredible crosses, he had created twenty-four goalscoring chances for his teammates. Twenty-four! That made him the most creative player in the whole entire tournament, ahead of Belgium's Kevin De Bruyne and Eden Hazard, and even ahead of Brazil's Neymar.

Not only that but Kieran was also now England's most famous free-kick king since his childhood hero, David Beckham. He had become only the third player to ever score for his country in a World Cup semi-final. The other two? Legends Sir Bobby Charlton and Gary Lineker.

'Not bad for a boy from Bury!' his brother Kelvin joked.

CHAPTER 2

A BACK GARDEN IN BURY

In a back garden in Bury, two brothers were playing football together. Or, to be more accurate, one brother was dribbling with a football and his younger brother was chasing after him, round and round in circles. Despite all his brother's tricks and flicks, the little boy kept going. He wanted the ball and he wasn't giving up.

'Come on, Kelvin, no-one likes a show-off!' their dad, Chris Trippier, called out from the back door. 'Stop teasing Kieran, and let him have a touch.'

'Fine, here you go,' Kelvin sighed, passing the ball to his younger brother.

As it rolled towards him, Kieran's eyes lit up like

he had just discovered gold. Finally, the ball was his! Carefully, he controlled it and then kicked it back with the side of his right foot. Kelvin looked very surprised when it landed at his feet.

'Hey, that was pretty good! For a six-year-old, I mean.'

That was the highest praise that Kieran had ever heard from his brother. He tried to act cool but inside, he was beaming with pride.

Kelvin was four years older, and Kieran was desperate to copy everything he did, especially when it came to playing football. All those hours of following his brother's fancy footwork around the back garden had been worth it, and all of those hours of practising on his own too. He was now 'pretty good'!

This time, rather than trying another trick on his own, Kelvin passed the ball back to Kieran. He had passed the test. How exciting – now, the two brothers were really playing football together! After a few simple passes, Kelvin decided to make it more of a challenge.

'Nice, now let's try to do it faster!' he said, pinging

the ball across the grass at top speed.

Woah! At first, Kieran couldn't quite control his brother's powerful passes. The ball kept bouncing off his foot or flying straight past it. However, by keeping his eye on the ball, he soon got the hang of it.

'Nice, now let's try one touch!' Kelvin said.

Woah! At first, Kieran's passes went all over the place – high, low, left, right, anywhere except the spot where Kelvin was standing. It was a good thing that the back garden had a high fence. However, by keeping his eye on the ball, he soon got the hang of it.

'Nice, now let's try longer balls!' his brother added, moving further away.

Woah! This was a totally different challenge for Kieran. The side-foot was good for short, accurate passes but now he needed to really *boot* the ball. It was time to try kicking with the front of his foot instead.

Again, at first, Kieran's passes went all over the place – high, low, left, right, anywhere except the spot where Kelvin was standing. However, by keeping his eye on the ball, he soon got the hang of it.

'Nice!'

When their dad came outside to watch, the brothers were fizzing long, first-time passes across the back garden to each other. As a football coach himself, Chris was very impressed, especially with his youngest son. Where had he learned to strike the ball so cleanly?

'Wow, you're a natural, Kieran!' he said.

First his brother, and now his dad – everyone was praising his football skills today! Kieran was delighted. With every pass, he was getting better and better.

'The Neville brothers better watch out for you two!' their dad joked.

Gary and Phil Neville were the new star full-backs for Chris's favourite football club, Manchester United. Together with Ryan Giggs, David Beckham, Paul Scholes and Eric Cantona, they were taking the Premier League by storm. And best of all, the Neville brothers were from Bury too.

'No thanks,' Kieran replied, without taking his eyes off the ball. 'I want to be a winger like Becks!'

'Come and join in, Dad!' Kelvin suggested.

'Oh, go on then!'

TRIPPIER

When it came to football, Chris never needed much persuading. Kieran and Kelvin's two-person passing game was now a three-person passing game, and it soon became a five-person game when their brothers, Chris Jr and Curtis, arrived.

Kieran was having the best time ever but five footballers in one small back garden? It was a recipe for disaster!

'What on earth is going on?'

Eleanor had just got home from work, and she didn't know whether to laugh or cry. Why couldn't her family play football somewhere else? There was a park just down the road but instead, her husband and sons had turned the back garden into a bombsite. There were plant-pots and paint cans lying everywhere.

'Uh-oh!' Kieran thought to himself, looking down at the ground guiltily. They were in big trouble.

'Watch out!' Kelvin called out suddenly.

Eleanor ducked just in time. The football sailed over her head, bounced off the fence and landed right in the middle of her favourite flowers.

'Sorry, Mum!'

CHAPTER 3

CITY OVER UNITED

That back-garden ball game was just the start of the family football coaching. Soon, Kieran was the star of his dad's local youth team, Seedfield. Playing on the right wing, he set up goal after goal with his dangerous deliveries.

'Close that boy down!' opposition coaches shouted whenever he got the ball. 'Don't let him cross it!'

Kieran loved playing for Seedfield. Football was even more fun when he had teammates to play with, and opponents to play against. It also helped that Seedfield won almost every match.

However, it wasn't long before bigger clubs were watching him. At the age of eight, Kieran was scouted by Manchester United. Manchester United! When they offered him a trial, Chris was the proudest parent in the whole entire world.

'My boy's going to be the new David Beckham!' he boasted to all of his mates.

'No pressure, eh?' Eleanor said to her husband with a smile. 'At least wait until he actually signs a contract or something!'

Training at 'The Cliff' was both an exciting and nerve-wracking experience for Kieran. After all, he was following in some very famous footsteps.

'This is where Becks and Giggsy started out,' he kept thinking to himself as he raced around the pitch. 'And who knows, maybe Sir Alex Ferguson is watching me from his office window right now!'

United weren't, however, the only top club watching Kieran. Their local rivals, Manchester City, also scouted him and invited him for a trial.

'Don't you dare become a Blue!' his United-mad family teased. 'Why would you want to go there anyway? They're rubbish!'

While the Red Devils were flying high, winning

trophy after trophy, the Sky Blues had been relegated from the Premier League all the way down to League One. Despite that, Kieran was determined to give it a go. A couple of his friends already played for the City academy and they loved it there.

'Good luck!' Chris called out as he dropped Kieran off at Platt Lane. Yes, he loved United, but he loved his son even more! All he wanted was for him to be happy, even if that meant playing for the enemies.

'So, how did it go?' Chris asked when he picked him up.

After sessions at United, Kieran was usually pretty quiet on the drive home. He just sat there in the passenger seat, worrying about every little mistake – a poor pass, a missed tackle, a shot off target.

After that first session at City, however, he couldn't stop talking.

'It was so much fun! I was on the same team as Danny and Sam. Remember them?'

'Yes, I—'

'Anyway, so we're about to kick off and the other boys are walking around as if they've already won

the game. No chance, we played them off the park.
You should have seen their faces!'

'Did you sco—?'

'A couple, but mainly I was setting them up for Sam
and our striker, Billy. By the end, the coach was calling
me "Becks" because my crossing was so good!'

'Well done, son!' his dad replied. 'So, what
happens n—'

'They want me to come back next week!' he
cheered, nearly jumping out of his car seat.

If Kieran was happy, then his dad was happy. It
was as simple as that. Chris would just have to get
used to the idea of having a son who played for City.

At least, Platt Lane was nearer to Bury. Chris often
spent long weeks working far from home in order to
earn enough money to feed his four growing sons.
If Eleanor was ever too busy to drive Kieran to City
training, he could always take the bus.

Kieran quickly settled into his new home at City.
He felt comfortable there, playing with his friends
and working with the youth coaches. Jim Cassell and
Steve Eyre loved working with Kieran too. He was

a fast learner and a real talent. In all their years of experience, they had rarely seen a nine-year-old kid who could strike the ball so cleanly, accurately and powerfully.

'He's got great vision, even in an eight-a-side game,' they discussed. 'Imagine how good he'll be once he moves up to a full-size pitch!'

Even at the age of nine, Kieran had big plans for his football future.

First, he would become City's wing wizard, racing down the right at Maine Road with 30,000 fans chanting his name.

Then, he would become England's wing wizard, and help his country to win the World Cup! He had watched the 1998 tournament on TV with his dad, and it had made a big impression on him.

Chris was England's biggest fan and so every match of the tournament was an emotional rollercoaster with lots of highs and lows.

'No!' he groaned as Dan Petrescu scored a last-minute winner to make it Romania 2 England 1. He banged his fists against the arms of the sofa.

'Are you okay, Dad?' Kieran asked. He looked like he was in real pain.

'You'll get used to this, son,' he muttered grumpily. 'Our national team always let us down.'

But four days later, his mood had changed.

'Yes!' Chris cried out as David Beckham scored a fantastic free kick to make it England 2 Colombia 0. 'We could go on and win this tournament!'

Kieran watched that free kick over and over again, as many times as he could. He couldn't help it; it was one of the best goals that he'd ever seen. The power, the curl, the dip, and then the celebration! Beckham raced over to the fans, pumping his fists and roaring.

'What a hero!' Kieran thought to himself.

England's second-round match against Argentina had even more ups and downs. There was no chance of his dad sitting still through all the drama. His right leg kept kicking the air as if he was out there playing on the pitch.

'Come on, England!'

Gabriel Batistuta scored a penalty, but then so did Alan Shearer. 1–1!

'Yes!' Chris cried out as Michael Owen scored a wondergoal. 2–1!

'No!' he groaned as Javier Zanetti equalised just before half-time. 2–2!

'NO!' father and son shouted at the screen together as the referee sent Beckham off for kicking out at Diego Simeone.

When the match went to penalties, Kieran could hardly bear to watch.

'We've got no chance here, son,' Chris declared miserably.

His dad was right. First Paul Ince missed and then David Batty. England were knocked out.

For a few minutes, both father and son sat there on the sofa in silence. Then Chris got up and switched off the TV.

'What did I tell you?' he said as he left the room. 'They always let us down in the end.'

'No, not always!' Kieran thought to himself. One day, he was going to prove his dad wrong. He would be Beckham without the red card, and lead England to World Cup glory.

CHAPTER 4

THE HOLCOMBE BROOK HERO

When Kieran wasn't starring for the Manchester City academy, he was starring for his primary school team instead. His life was already football, football, football – all day every day! There was some important education in between, of course. His parents made sure of that.

'If we hear that you've been misbehaving in class,' Eleanor warned him, 'there'll be no football for you, okay?'

'Okay, Mum. I'll be good, I promise!' Kieran replied with a panicked look on his face. The fear of no football was more than enough to keep him out of trouble.

Kieran loved playing with his school friends. It was like being back at Seedfield, with lots of laughs at training, and at the back of the team bus on away trips. They always wanted to win, but it wasn't as serious as it was at the City academy.

Still, with Kieran flying down the wing, Holcombe Brook flew all the way to the Bury Schools' Cup Final. There were other good players in the team, but Kieran was head and shoulders above the rest. He might be joking around with his mates in the warm-up but once the whistle blew, his smile disappeared. It was game-time, and Kieran had to win, no matter what.

Losing just wasn't an option. If he didn't score the goal, he almost always set it up with one of his incredible free kicks or crosses. Could he now lead his school to one last, important victory?

'Best of luck today, Kieran!' the headmaster called out to him as he jogged onto the field to warm up. 'How are you feeling?'

'I'm feeling good thanks, Mr Howarth!' he replied, sounding as calm as ever.

For some of the Holcombe Brook players, the final would be the biggest game of their lives. That was a lot of pressure for ten-year-olds to deal with.

For Kieran, however, it was just the latest in a long line of big games. After all, he had been on trial with Manchester United at The Cliff, playing on the same pitch as Becks and Giggsy, and now he played for Manchester City. So, the Bury Schools' Cup Final? No, there was no reason to feel nervous about that. Kieran was just going to go out there, enjoy himself, and win.

'Come on, boys!' he cheered confidently before kick-off. 'We can do this!'

The Holcombe Brook players pulled up their socks and got stuck in. If Kieran said they could win it, then they could win it. He was their leader, as well as their superstar.

'Go on, son!' Kieran's parents shouted out on the sidelines. Kelvin was there too, to cheer his younger brother on towards the trophy.

Every time Kieran got the ball, the crowd held their breath. Holcombe Brook hoped for a goal, and their opponents feared the worst. Kieran was dominating the game in midfield, using his right foot like a dangerous weapon. What would he do next – a killer cross, a deadly dribble, a perfect pass, a stunning strike? He was capable of anything.

'Keep going, Kieran!' his coach encouraged him.

It was a very exciting final, full of fast, end-to-end football. There could only be one winner, though, and who would it be? What Holcombe Brook needed was a calm head, someone who could produce a real moment of magic...

Kieran got the ball in his own half and dribbled forward. As he looked up for a teammate to pass to, he spotted that the opposition goalkeeper was off his line. Should he? Why not?! It was definitely worth a try. If Becks could do it for Manchester United against Wimbledon, then why couldn't he score from the halfway line too? If it worked, Kieran would go down in Bury Schools' history...

In a flash, he pulled back his right foot and aimed for goal. BANG! As the ball sailed through the air, everyone held their breath and watched. Surely not?!

The keeper turned and sprinted back towards his goal but he was too late to stop it from landing in the back of the net.

Goooooooooooooooooooaaaaaaaaaaaaaaaaalllllllllllll lllllllllllllll!!!!!!!!!!!!!!!!!!!!!

What a strike, what a feeling! Kieran was the Holcombe Brook hero yet again. With the pressure on, he had scored an absolute worldie! He ran around punching the air, until his teammates piled on top of him.

'Yes, mate!'

'You legend!'

'We're the Champions!'

On the sidelines, his family swapped big hugs and big grins. They were so proud of their little match-winner.

'Well done, Kieran!' they cried out.

After the trophy presentation, his teammates lifted their hero up into the air and carried him around the pitch. With a winners' medal around his neck and the Bury Schools' Cup in his hands, Kieran felt on top of the world.

If only he could score the winning goal in cup finals every day! He could never get bored of the buzz. Oh well, there would just have to be many more triumphs ahead; Kieran would make sure of that.

Eventually, the celebrations had to end, and everyone walked back to their cars to drive home. They might not have said it out loud but they were all thinking the same thing – his teammates, his opponents, his family, the Holcombe Brook headmaster:

'That boy has a very bright football future ahead of him!'

CHAPTER 5

SET PIECES AT CITY

At Manchester City, youth coaches Jim Cassell and Steve Eyre were thinking exactly the same thing. Kieran was well on his way to becoming a top professional footballer. He ticked all the right boxes:

✓ **He had a fantastic family around him.**

Chris and Eleanor were there cheering Kieran on at every academy match, and so were his grandparents. The City coaches knew just how important that love and support was for a promising young player. There would be plenty of times ahead when Kieran would need a hug, or some words of advice. Plus, his grandma was always there to keep his feet on the ground.

'What's wrong with you, lad? Get stuck in!' she often shouted on the sidelines. If Kieran had a bad game, she was never shy to tell him so.

✓ **He had terrific talent.**

Kieran's touch and technique were excellent, week in, week out. It was rare to see such a consistent young player. He wasn't a typical tricky winger, amazing one minute, and awful the next. Instead, he worked hard for his team and kept things simple.

'That's it – one touch to control it, then look up and CROSS!'

Kieran's remarkable right foot was deadlier than ever now that he was playing on bigger pitches. Defenders just couldn't deal with his lovely long balls and crosses. He could find the danger zone every time.

✓ **He had amazing ambition.**

Kieran wasn't content with just becoming a professional footballer. Of course, that would be a great achievement, but he was aiming a lot higher than that. He wanted to be a superstar for Manchester City *and* England!

By 2002, City were back in the Premier League, and their manager Kevin Keegan was giving lots of his young players a chance to shine. Shaun Wright-Phillips, Joey Barton, Stephen Jordan... the list went on and on.

'That will be me soon!' Kieran declared. He would do whatever it took to make his dream come true.

✓ **He was a confident character.**

Yes, Kieran liked to practise the same pass again and again until it was perfect, but he certainly wasn't a right-foot robot! He was competitive and mischievous, and that's what Jim and Steve liked most about him.

'Confidence,' the City youth coach called it. 'You don't get anywhere in this sport without it!'

Jim lived near the Trippiers and he knew their neighbourhood well. It wasn't an easy place to grow up and, without the right guidance, good kids could lose their way and get into trouble. The City youth coach was determined to make sure that didn't happen to Kieran.

'If you live right, you'll make it!' Jim kept telling him.

He often dropped Kieran home at the end of training, but only after he had completed his favourite football challenge.

'Right, first to twenty?' Steve said, grabbing a big bag of balls.

'You don't give up, do you, Coach?' Kieran replied cheekily. 'Fine, if you're ready to get beaten again...'

Steve was left-footed and Kieran was right-footed, so they took it in turns to shoot from either side of the D. The challenge was simple – the first person to score twenty free kicks was the winner. They could usually find a young goalkeeper who was up for some extra shot-stopping.

'Go!'

Kieran took five steps backwards in a diagonal line away from the ball. When he was even younger, he used to copy Beckham's run-up and arm-swing, but now he preferred to do things his own way. He ran forward confidently and kicked the ball with plenty of power, lift and curl.

There wasn't a group of big, brave defenders in front of Kieran but he always pretended that there was. That was the first part of scoring a free kick. Somehow, he had to get the ball past the wall, whether it went over them, around them, or even under them if they jumped!

The second part was getting the ball past the keeper. To do that, Kieran needed power, but above all, he needed accuracy. Most shots near the middle of the goal would be easy to save. Instead, he had to find one of the four corners: top left, bottom left, top right or bottom right.

Becoming a free-kick king took lots of talent and practice. Kieran had the talent and he was always willing to put in the practice.

'Yes!' he cried out, throwing his arms up in the air. 'Sorry, Coach, can I just check the score – am I really winning this *8–1*? This is getting embarrassing for you!'

Steve sent another free kick flying high over the crossbar. 'Hmmm, it's not my day today.'

'It never is, Coach!'

Occasionally, however, Kieran's confident character got him into a bit of trouble.

One day, the groundsman at Platt Lane came storming into Steve's office. He wasn't happy at all.

'It keeps happening and I won't stand for it!' he muttered angrily. 'Whoever it is, needs to stop RIGHT NOW!'

The City youth coach had no idea what the groundsman was talking about. 'Sorry, what keeps happening?'

'When I'm out there on the lawnmower, one of those pesky kids keeps kicking footballs at my head! But by the time I turn around, he's disappeared. He thinks he's clever but when I catch him—'

'Ok, I'm really sorry about that,' Steve said, trying to calm the groundsman down. 'I'm going to find out who's doing it and when I do, they'll be punished, I promise!'

The City youth coach knew exactly who the troublemaker was, but he didn't have the heart to punish him properly. A warning would be enough.

'If you don't find a new way to practise your long passing,' Steve told Kieran with a smile on his face, 'then I'll have to tell that groundsman where you live!'

CHAPTER 6

HERO AT HOME

Kieran wasn't the only successful footballer in his family. He was following in his brother's footsteps once more. Kelvin was working his way up through the ranks at Oldham Athletic. 'The Latics' played in League One and, at the age of seventeen, he was already training with the first team.

'It's so cool – you're going to make your senior debut soon!' Kieran said excitedly.

Years after those first back-garden games, he was still Kelvin's biggest fan. He looked up to his brother for advice about everything. It was pretty cool to have his hero right there at home with him!

When he was bored, Kieran would knock on his

brother's bedroom door with a ball in his hands.

'Fancy a kickabout outside?'

'Oh, go on then!' Kelvin usually said. When it came to football, he never needed much persuading.

Kieran always looked forward to playing with his brother because he gave him lots of great tips. They could talk about the best free kick technique for hours! It was part of Kieran's football education. He wanted to know everything about everything.

'Can I come and watch you train today?' Kieran asked.

'*Again*?' his brother rolled his eyes. 'Ok, but don't embarrass me in front of my new teammates!'

Kieran loved to watch the Oldham sessions. Whenever Kelvin let him, he was there on the sidelines, taking it all in. Kieran went to all of his brother's matches too, but he preferred the practices. For a football-mad thirteen-year-old, it was like a sneak peek into his future. This was what being a professional player was really like.

There were lots of jokes! 'A happy team is a successful team,' Jim often told them at the City academy and that seemed to be true at Oldham. The players loved to mess around, especially when the manager wasn't looking. Sometimes, they tried silly skills, sometimes they took stupid shots, and sometimes, they just kicked balls at each other.

'That's the sort of thing we do at school!' Kieran thought to himself. He couldn't wait to be part of the City first team, training together every day.

There were lots of drills! Kieran loved finding ways to improve. He kept a close eye on each training exercise – running, passing, crossing, shooting, one vs one, three vs three, piggy in the middle. If Kelvin hadn't forced him to leave his kit at home, Kieran would have jumped over the fence and joined in!

There were lots of tactics! That was one of the biggest changes from junior to senior level. Suddenly, it was all so organised. There was a plan for absolutely everything, from defending corners on the left, to attacking free kicks on the right.

'How do you remember all of the manager's instructions?' Kieran asked Kelvin on the way home.

His brother shrugged. 'Practice,' was all he said.

It certainly seemed to be working. Kelvin was getting closer and closer to his Oldham debut. After one game on the bench, he played the last thirty-five minutes away at Brentford in October 2004.

'Congratulations!' Kieran was cheering before Kelvin even got through the front door. 'What did it feel like when you came on?'

His brother shrugged like it was just another football match. 'Good,' was all he said.

Over the next few weeks, Kelvin became a regular in the Oldham defence. He was a speedy right-back, who could also play on the left.

'Just like Phil Neville!' their dad liked to say. Even though his youngest son played for City, Chris was still a massive Manchester United fan.

Kieran never missed a chance to cheer on Kelvin at Oldham's home ground, Boundary Park. He was so proud of his brilliant brother, the professional footballer. He was now playing in a proper stadium in front of thousands of cheering fans. If Kelvin could do it, then so could Kieran! His brother's success made him more determined than ever.

CHAPTER 7

THE WOODHEY HIGH HERO

Kieran's sporting success didn't stop once he got to secondary school. No, it just kept growing and growing! That was largely thanks to Mr Garcka, his cool new PE teacher at Woodhey High.

'I know you love football, but we play lots of different sports here,' he explained when Kieran arrived in Year 7. 'Would you be interested in trying something new?'

More competitions, and more chances of winning? Yes please! Kieran loved that idea. He was willing to give anything a go.

'You're really fast. What about running?' Mr Garcka suggested.

So, Kieran joined the school cross-country team. To this day, over ten years later, he still holds the Woodhey High record for the fastest 400 metres!

'You've got a lovely right foot, but what about a sport where you use your hands instead?' Mr Garcka suggested.

So, Kieran joined the school basketball team! Just like in football, he dribbled forward and set up lots of chances to score.

'You're a great team player, but what about a one vs one sport instead?' Mr Garcka suggested.

So, Kieran joined the school table tennis team! Just like in football, he had to make sure that every single shot was accurate and aimed at the corners.

Between Manchester City and all his new extra activities, Kieran hardly had a spare minute to relax. That was probably for the best, though, his parents, teachers and coaches all agreed. As long as he was busy, he was keeping out of trouble.

'If you live right, you will make it' – that's what Jim always told him.

Kieran enjoyed learning lots of new skills from

all his new sports, but nothing would ever compare to football. It would always be his favourite, no matter what.

'Don't worry, I won't be swapping footie for ping-pong anytime soon!' he joked with Jim.

Kieran was still progressing well at the City academy but Mr Garcka wanted to make sure that his student had a Plan B, just in case things didn't work out. So many fifteen-year-old footballers were released by their clubs, with broken hearts and no career plans. The PE teacher really didn't want Kieran to be one of them.

'If you couldn't be a football player, what would you want to be?' Mr Garcka asked.

Kieran shrugged. He was so sure that he would achieve his dream that he hadn't really thought about it.

'What about being a football coach?'

Like Jim and Steve? Sure, that would be fun! Kieran was always looking to improve himself, so maybe he would be good at helping others to improve too.

'Brilliant, I'll sign you up!' Mr Garcka told him as he walked away.

'Wait a minute, sir. Sign me up for what?'

Mr Garcka had signed Kieran up for his first coaching qualification. The teacher divided a big group of ten-year-olds into teams to compete in a mini-World Cup. Each team would be managed by one of Woodhey High's bright young coaches.

'Yes, we're England!' Kieran cheered patriotically. 'We're definitely going to win the World Cup now.'

He didn't have much time to work with his new team. 'What would Jim and Steve do?' he kept thinking. After a few passing and shooting drills, Kieran gave each player a position that he thought would suit their skills best. His main message, however, was aimed at the whole team – work together and you'll win.

'Good luck!' he shouted as they took to the pitch for their first match. 'Enjoy it!'

By working together, Kieran's team battled all the way to the final, and then all the way to a dreaded penalty shoot-out.

'Now, I really wish we weren't England!' Kieran muttered to himself.

He thought about the defeat to Argentina at the 1998 World Cup, but also the more recent defeat to Portugal at Euro 2004. What was it that his dad had said? 'England always let you down in the end.' No, Kieran was determined to be the manager who ended nearly forty years of hurt.

'Just take your time and try your best,' he encouraged each of his worried young players before they stepped up. He knew what he was talking about. He was his school's penalty taker and he hadn't missed a single one. 'Remember, you've done so well to get this far!'

With their young manager's support, England did it – they lifted the World Cup trophy! Kieran was delighted, and so was his PE teacher.

'You did an excellent job with those kids,' Mr Garcka congratulated him. 'You'll make a great football coach one day!'

For now, though, Kieran was fully focused on being a great football player. The City academy had asked him not to play for his school but he couldn't help himself. Woodhey High needed him! Whenever he could, he raced back from training just in time to catch the school team bus.

Mr Garcka was always relieved to see Kieran. 'Phew, I didn't think you were going to make it today!'

'No chance, I wouldn't miss it for the world, Sir!'

In his final year, Kieran helped Woodhey High to reach the Bury Schools' Cup Final, just like he had with Holcombe Brook Primary. Could he win the double? Yes, and not only that, but he also scored a stunning hat-trick in the final!

From his own half, he dribbled past one defender, then another, then another, then another, before beating the keeper.

Gooooooooooooooooooooaaaaaaaaaaaaaaaaalllllllllllll llllllllllllllll!!!!!!!!!!!!!!!!!!!

As a clearance came out to him, he struck the ball sweetly on the volley, straight into the top corner.

Gooooooooooooooooooooaaaaaaaaaaaaaaaaalllllllllllll llllllllllllllll!!!!!!!!!!!!!!!!!!!

From the edge of the box, he curled a shot into the back of the net.

Gooooooooooooooooooooaaaaaaaaaaaaaaaallllllllllll llllllllllllllll!!!!!!!!!!!!!!!!!!!!

Kieran punched the air and hugged his teammates. What a way to become the Woodhey High hero! He had yet another winners' medal to add to his collection. Kieran was really living up to his name as 'The Bury Beckham'.

CHAPTER 8

RIGHT WING TO RIGHT-BACK

By the age of 16, Kieran was spending more and more hours on the training field at Platt Lane. The closer he got to the Manchester City first team, the more he needed to up his game. There were so many talented young players at the club, all competing for a small number of professional contracts.

'Don't worry, you're on the right track,' Jim and Steve reassured Kieran.

Michael Johnson and Daniel Sturridge were the latest young stars to come out of the academy. They had just led City all the way to the final of the 2006 FA Youth Cup. Michael was a box-to-box midfielder who loved to pass, while Daniel was a skilful striker who loved to shoot.

What did Kieran have that would help him stand out from the crowd? He was good at taking free kicks but would that be enough?

'No, I need more than just that,' he told his family. 'Even Becks doesn't get in the England team just because of that. I need a special talent that I can use all the time.'

Aha, got it! Kieran would be a hard-working winger who loved to cross. His right foot was already really good and with practice, practice, practice, he would make it even better.

After most training sessions, Kieran would go back out with Steve and a big bag of balls. They still played first-to-twenty free kicks from time to time, but usually, Kieran now preferred practising cross after cross. There were so many different match situations to prepare for.

Steve was always setting him new challenges. It was like being in the back garden in Bury with Kelvin all over again.

'Cross it early! Hit it first time on the run and aim for the six-yard box.'

'This time, take a touch and then curl the ball high to the back post.'

'Next, dribble forward a few yards before fizzing it into the front post area.'

Sometimes, Steve wouldn't say anything at all. He would just make a late run into the box and call for the cross. 'Now!'

Every time he pulled his right foot back to kick the ball, Kieran had so many different things to think about – the timing of the cross, the height, the power, the angle, the curve. It sounded so complicated but Steve was right; it was actually pretty simple:

'If you keep delivering the ball into the danger zone, then eventually, someone's got to score!'

Thanks to all his extra hard work, Kieran's crossing became more and more consistent from every possible angle. Jim and Steve both still believed in 'The Bury Beckham' 100 per cent but they were having second thoughts about what his best position might be.

Was Kieran really a right winger, after all? He didn't have fancy footwork like Aaron Lennon, or Manchester United's new star, Cristiano Ronaldo. Plus, not all teams played with wingers anymore. The classic 4–4–2 was being replaced by new football formations. There was the 3–5–2, the 4–3–3, the 4–2–3–1...

Where else could Kieran play on the pitch? What if they turned him into a right-back instead? Gary Neville played there for Manchester United and he was a great crosser too. From further back, Kieran would have even more time and space to put brilliant balls into the box.

Plus, being a full-back wasn't such a boring job anymore. It was now a fun position, with lots more freedom to get involved in the game. Ashley Cole at Chelsea, for example, used his speed to attack all the time! Kieran could make those overlapping runs too.

'It's worth a go,' Jim and Steve decided after lots of discussion.

Kieran was more than happy to try a different position. If it got him into the City first team, he would try absolutely anything!

'I might be a bit small to be a goalkeeper, though!' he joked.

Kieran knew exactly who to talk to about becoming a right-back – his hero at home! Kelvin couldn't help laughing when he first heard the news.

'You don't have to copy me in every single way, you know!'

'As if! Don't flatter yourself.'

The brothers began practising in the back garden, until their mum asked them to play in the park instead.

Kieran had lots to learn about defending. Marking, tackling, blocking, heading – they were all things that he used to do as a winger, but now they were much more important. He was going to need plenty of help from his teammates and coaches.

'That's your man, Tripps!' Kieran's friend, Ben Mee, called out from centre-back. 'Track him!'

'Get tighter!' Steve screamed from the sidelines. 'Stop the cross!'

It was a steep learning curve for Kieran but minute

by minute and mistake by mistake, he was becoming less of a right winger and more of a right-back.

Jim and Steve were delighted with their decision. 'At this rate, it looks like we've found City's Number 2 for the next fifteen years!'

CHAPTER 9

HEROES AT UNITED

Growing up in the Greater Manchester area, Kieran couldn't help supporting Sir Alex Ferguson's United team, especially having a dad like Chris.

'United!' he cheered when they first won the Premier League in 1993,

'United!' he cheered when they won the double in 1996,

'United!' he cheered when they won the treble in 1999,

And 'United!' he was still cheering when they won their tenth Premier League title in 2008.

By then, Kieran's first Manchester United hero had left the club. David Beckham was every boy's idol, with his football skills and boy-band good looks. But for a young right winger like Kieran, he was extra special.

He copied the way Becks struck his fantastic free kicks.

He copied the way Becks curled in his incredible crosses.

He copied the way Becks looked up and picked out a perfect long pass.

Kieran copied Becks' shaved head and he had even copied Becks' Wimbledon wonder-strike when he scored from the halfway line for Holcombe Brook Primary in the Bury Schools' Cup final.

When people gave him the nickname 'The Bury Beckham', it was the proudest moment of his life!

But when Kieran changed his position, he changed his hero too. He was a right-back now and luckily, Manchester United also had a brilliant right-back. Best of all, he was even born in Bury!

'What did I say all those years ago?' Kieran's dad laughed. 'I told you that you and Kelvin would be the new Neville brothers!'

Gary Neville didn't have as much style as his best friend Becks, but he made up for that with his passion and dedication. No-one fought harder than Neville for United. He was always organising his teammates and urging them on until the final whistle.

'Why do you like him?' Kieran's friends always asked. 'He's so boring and all he does is shout!'

'That's not true – you don't win eight Premier League titles and two Champions Leagues for being good at shouting!'

Or all those England caps either. Gary Neville had played for his country eighty-five times, at two World Cups and three European Championships. That was Kieran's biggest dream of all – to play for England at major tournaments. So alongside his brother Kelvin, Neville was a pretty awesome hero to have.

Kieran watched him carefully whenever United were on TV. If he wanted to become City's next right-back, Kieran needed to improve his defending, and Neville was one of the best defenders around. He wasn't the quickest or the strongest, but he was one of the smartest. He never lost his concentration, and he was always in the right place at the right time. Neville battled bravely for every header, block and tackle.

'You'd really hate to play against him, wouldn't you?' his dad said with a smile.

'Yes,' Kieran agreed enthusiastically. 'I hope people say that about me too one day!'

He had a long list of things that he admired about Neville, but the top three were:

1. His leadership!

Neville did spend a lot of time shouting, but that was only because he wanted to win so much. And it worked because he inspired his United teammates to keep winning trophy after trophy. Kieran tried to show that same passion when he was out there on the pitch for City.

2. His decision-making!

Neville always seemed to know when to defend and when to attack. But how did he know? That was something that Kieran was still working hard on with his coaches at City.

3. His energy!

Neville never stopped running up and down the pitch, all game long. When he got the chance to go forward, he kept things simple, just like Kieran did. He looked up to see who was in the box and then delivered a dangerous cross.

'He can't bend it like Beckham but he puts the ball in the right area every time!' Kieran argued.

And how did Neville become so good at crossing? With practice, practice, practice. By spending even longer on the training ground, Kieran hoped to one day reach that highest level. He was determined.

Meanwhile, Jim and Steve were working on new nicknames for him:

'The New Neville?'

'The City Cafu?'

'No, nothing beats The Bury Beckham!'

CHAPTER 10

YOUTH CUP WINNER

Manchester City hadn't won the FA Youth Cup since 1986, before Kieran was even born! By the time he joined the club's Under-18s, it was twenty-two years later, but after signing his first professional contract, he was feeling even more confident than usual.

'Come on lads, this is going to be our year!'

'Yeah!' his teammates roared.

City had a very strong side: Kieran, Ben and Dedryck Boyata at the back, with Vladimír Weiss on the wing, and Daniel up front. Daniel was now playing for the first team too but he had unfinished business in the FA Youth Cup. He had suffered a painful defeat to Liverpool in the final two years earlier.

'Not this time!' Daniel vowed.

City powered their way past Millwall, Reading, Bristol City and Plymouth Argyle. Kieran raced down the right, curling in incredible cross after incredible cross. The team scored lots of goals, and they didn't concede many either.

'Great work, lads!' Jim clapped and cheered on the sidelines.

The coach was delighted with his young players. They were doing the club proud. With a 2–1 win over Jordan Henderson's Sunderland, City were into the FA Youth Cup final again.

Their last opponents would be the toughest of all – Chelsea! Their owner, Roman Abramovich, was a billionaire and he had invested lots of money in the club's academy. Not only had Chelsea built the best training facilities in England, but they had also spent millions on buying the best young players from all over the world. How were City's local boys supposed to compete with that?

'You've got nothing to fear!' Jim told his players before kick-off at Stamford Bridge. 'You've all worked so hard to get here. Now, you're only two games away from winning the cup. Go out there and get the job done!'

Jim had full faith in his players. His academy was developing one first-team star after another: Shaun Wright-Phillips, Joey Barton, Micah Richards, Daniel... the list went on and on. Jim was constantly telling the manager, Sven-Göran Eriksson, about his next top talents.

City's Number 2 was one of them, and he certainly wasn't worried about playing in a Premier League stadium in front of thousands of fans. No, Kieran was absolutely buzzing ahead of his big day! He wanted to compete at the highest level possible, and that's exactly what he was doing.

From the Bury Schools' Cup final, Kieran had fought his way to the FA Youth Cup final. He had been the Holcombe Brook hero and then the Woodhey High hero. Could he now become the Manchester City hero too?

Kieran calmly dribbled past Gaël Kakuta, the Chelsea winger, and played a brilliant ball down the line to Daniel. He cut inside and tested the goalkeeper with a swerving strike.

'Good stuff, lads!' Jim shouted. 'More of that!'

Kieran, however, had defending to do. Kakuta attacked at speed, weaving one way and then the other. The winger's feet danced but Kieran didn't dive in. He watched and waited until... SLIDE TACKLE!

'Well done, Tripps!' Ben cheered and the City fans roared.

Kieran smiled proudly. All his hard work with Steve was really paying off. He was earning that 'New Neville' nickname. He ran up and down the right, all game long, helping his team out at both ends of the pitch.

In the end, the first leg finished in a 1–1 draw. That result left City in a great position to win the FA Youth Cup in the second leg back home at the Etihad. They would have to do it without their goalscorer, Daniel, however. He was now City's starting striker in the Premier League.

'Good luck – bring it home, boys!' he told his teammates.

Despite letting in an early own goal, City did just that. They showed their strong team spirit by bouncing back brilliantly. First, Ben scored a header and then City won a free kick within shooting range. Kieran was desperate to take it, but so was Vladimír.

'Fine, you can have this one,' Kieran muttered moodily, 'but you better score it!'

No problem! Vladimír stepped up and curled the ball around the wall and into the top corner. *GOAL!*

'I'm still taking the next one!' Kieran teased as they celebrated together in front of the fans.

With five minutes to go, David Ball scored a penalty to seal the victory. City were the 2008 FA Youth Cup winners!

Chelsea grew more and more frustrated as the clock ticked down, and in the last minute, one of their players flew in with a nasty, reckless tackle on Kieran.

'Argghhhh!' he screamed out in agony.

Kieran had been excited about the after-match party, but sadly, he wouldn't be there to enjoy it; he had to leave the pitch on a stretcher and miss out on all the fun. He missed out on the confetti, the cheering, the dancing, and most importantly of all, the lifting of the trophy.

But he refused to let that bad luck bring him down. At the age of seventeen, he had just played an important role in City's biggest achievement for years. With the winners' medal around his neck, it felt like the future was his to reach out and grab with both hands.

Next step: the first team. Kieran was now ready to become City's new right-back.

When Jim next saw Eriksson walking down the corridor, he called out confidently, 'Don't worry, we've got lots more academy lads coming your way soon!'

CHAPTER 11

A WORLD CUP TO FORGET

City's young right-back was soon England's young right-back too. And after only one cap for the Under-18s, Kieran moved straight up to the next level. He was flying!

The England Under-19s coach Brian Eastick was looking to strengthen his squad for the 2009 European Championship qualifying round, and City was always a good place to look. Daniel and Ben were now playing for the Under-20s but Kieran was a year younger than them. Plus, Eastick needed a new right-back.

'Congratulations!' Kieran's family cheered when he shared his exciting news. 'First the FA Youth Cup,

and now this – there's no stopping you. You'll be in
the England senior squad in no time!'

For now, though, Kieran was off to Northern
Ireland, where the Under-19s had three games in five
days. It was a good thing that he was used to playing
lots of football! He started the first two games, and
England won both of them. Then when Eastick
rested him against Serbia, the team got hammered
4–1.

'They're lost without you!' Kieran's family argued.

Despite that defeat, England were through to
the 2009 European Championships in the Ukraine.
Kieran couldn't wait to play in his first international
tournament. It was going to be a challenge and an
adventure. His City teammate Andrew Tutte was
going with him, and so were Danny Welbeck and
Danny Drinkwater from United.

'Manchester's finest!' they joked together.
Although they were rivals for their clubs, they were
teammates for their country.

England arrived at the tournament with high
expectations, so two draws in the first two games

was a very disappointing start. In the first match against Switzerland, they were on the verge of a 1–0 victory but they conceded a late equaliser. The second match against Ukraine finished 2–2.

'Come on, we have to win this last group game!' Eastick urged his players.

Unfortunately, Kieran had watched the first two games from the bench. The England manager had picked a speedy kid from Sheffield instead, called Kyle Walker. Against Slovenia, however, Eastick decided to take a risk. He moved Kyle to centre-back and brought Kieran in at right-back.

'No more of those rapid forward runs, okay, Walks?' Kieran teased. 'That's my job now!'

Although they were competing with each other, they got on really well. With Kieran and Kyle playing together, England ran riot.

In the tenth minute against Slovenia, Kieran won the ball on the right and dribbled forward. He passed to Nathan Delfouneso, who passed to Danny Welbeck, who flicked it back for Henri Lansbury to shoot. 1–0!

'It's great to have you back, Tripps!' Danny cheered as they celebrated a great team goal.

It was great to be back and that was only the beginning. They ended up thrashing Slovenia 7–1. After that, Eastick had no choice but to keep Kieran in the team!

England were through to the semi-finals, where they faced their old rivals France. After an awful start, they fought back bravely to win 3–1 in extra-time.

'We're in the final!' Kieran screamed, hugging their man of the match, Nathan.

Was Kieran about to add an Under-19 European Championship winner's medal to his collection? He hoped so.

England were feeling confident, even though they had to play the tournament hosts again. This time, with 25,000 locals cheering them on, Ukraine took an early lead from a corner-kick. Kieran was protecting the back post but the shot flew past the keeper at the front post. There was nothing Kieran could do except pick the ball out of the net and boot it downfield.

'Come on, heads up!' he shouted, doing his best Gary Neville impression. 'We're good enough to beat this lot!'

Kieran couldn't do anything about Dmytro Korkishko's fantastic free kick in the second half either. It was game, and tournament, over for England.

'We should have won that!' Kieran kept thinking, long after the final whistle had blown. They had let the pressure get to them.

'Unlucky lads,' Eastick told his devastated players. 'You've done so well to get this far and don't forget – we've got the Under-20 World Cup coming up in a few months!'

A World Cup! Kieran couldn't wait. He was in the squad that travelled to Egypt in September, but there was no Kyle, no Nathan, no Henri, and there were no Dannys either. Instead, Kieran found himself surrounded by his City youth teammates. Ben was back, Andrew was there, and several others had been called up too.

'It's like a club tour!' they joked.

The laughs didn't last very long, though, once the

tournament kicked off. For Kieran, it turned out to be a first World Cup to forget.

England held on for eighty-four minutes in their first match against Uruguay, until Tabaré Viúdez scored a stunning scissor-kick winner.

'How did we let that happen?' Kieran cried out, but his fellow defenders just slumped their shoulders and stared down at the grass.

Things got even worse in their next match against Ghana. Four of England's key players were too ill to play, but the others did their best to carry on. Kieran curled a lovely free kick into the box and Ben flicked it goal-wards… SMACK! The ball hit the crossbar.

'So close!' they both groaned with their hands on their heads.

After that, however, Ghana stormed forward in attack and England had no way of stopping them.

1–0, 2–0, 3–0, 4–0!

Kieran couldn't believe it. He trudged off the pitch in total despair. It was an absolute disaster! After all his hopes and expectations, his first World Cup was over already.

'Come on, we have to win this last group game!'
Eastick urged his players. One victory would at least
cheer them up a bit before the long journey home.

That team-talk had worked brilliantly at the
Under-19 Euros, but not this time – the best that
England could do was draw against Uzbekistan, and
they nearly lost again. Not only were they heading
home, but they also finished bottom of the group.

'What a nightmare!' Kieran thought to himself.
He couldn't wait to get back to Manchester City and
move on with his career. Then hopefully, one day,
he would get the chance to have a World Cup to
remember with England.

CHAPTER 12

STOP-START AT CITY

Back in 2008 when Kieran and his teammates
won the FA Youth Cup, Manchester City were the
underdogs and Chelsea were the rich boys. That was
all about to change, however.

Months later, City had a billionaire owner too, and
Sheikh Mansour was even richer than Abramovich.
He wanted to win the Premier League title as soon as
possible, no matter how much money that cost.

'Uh-oh, we're in trouble,' Kieran told Ben
gloomily.

It was potentially very bad news for the club's
young players. If City suddenly started spending lots
of money on international superstars, would the

homegrown boys every get the chance to play? All they could do was wait and see.

Soon, City had bought themselves a brand-new defence – Wayne Bridge on the left, Vincent Kompany and Tal Ben Haim in the middle, and Pablo Zabaleta on the right.

'Wow, that was quick!' Kieran gasped.

Kieran was still only eighteen but he was already itching to play proper first-team games. That now looked very unlikely at City. In Summer 2009, Kieran didn't go on the South Africa tour, and he didn't play in the Scottish friendlies against Rangers and Celtic either.

However, the City manager Mark Hughes did take him to Spain for the Joan Gamper Trophy game against Barcelona.

'It's now or never,' Kieran told himself. If he got the chance to play, he had to take it.

The atmosphere at the Nou Camp was out of this world. There were over 94,000 people there, just to watch a pre-season game. As he warmed up, Kieran couldn't help looking over at Barcelona's stars: Carles

Puyol, Thierry Henry, Zlatan Ibrahimović and, of course, Lionel Messi. What a team! Was he really about to share a pitch with them? It seemed too good to be true.

Kieran watched from the bench as City took the lead through Martin Petrov. The minutes ticked by, and still he sat there as a sub. Just as he began to give up hope, he got the call he was waiting for:

'Get ready, kid. You're coming on!'

Down on the touchline, Kieran took a long, deep breath. What a place to play your first-senior game! He was wearing Number 54 – was the shirt his now? No, he had to go out there and earn it first.

Before he ran on, Hughes gave him some final instructions. 'I want you to keep things tight in defence. Oh, and enjoy yourself!'

With ten minutes left, City were still 1–0 up. Kieran replaced Shaun Wright-Phillips to help out the right-back, Javier Garrido. He chased up and down the pitch, alert to every Barcelona pass.

Block! Interception! Tackle!

Before he knew it, the final whistle had blown and

Kieran was shaking hands with Messi and Zlatan.

'I'm never washing my hands again!' he laughed with Vladimír.

Kieran hoped that Barcelona game would be the start of something special. However, once the new Premier League season started, he was back playing for the City Under-23s again.

'I guess that's it, then,' he said grumpily.

It was so frustrating to get a brief taste of the big time, and then have it taken away like that. Kieran kept working hard, but he knew that he could learn so much more by playing proper league football. He wasn't getting any closer to the City first team; in fact, he was probably getting further away. Did Hughes even remember who he was anymore?

It didn't really matter because, by December, Hughes was no longer the manager. Kieran tried to impress the new boss, Roberto Mancini, but with City chasing the Premier League title, the young kids didn't stand a chance.

Jim and Steve could both see that Kieran was losing faith in his first team dream. If they didn't do something soon, City might end up losing one of their top young talents.

'What about sending him out on loan?' they suggested to the Under-23s manager, Glyn Hodges. 'The boy needs proper match experience.'

Hodges was happy with the idea, and so was Kieran. Whether at City, or elsewhere, Kieran just wanted to play professional football – week in week out.

CHAPTER 13

BARNSLEY AND BACK

Kieran was raring to go as he arrived at the Barnsley training ground. He was only joining The Tykes for one month, while their two regular right-backs recovered from injuries. However, if he played well, who knew? Maybe manager Mark Robins would want to keep him a bit longer.

'Welcome,' Robins said, shaking his hand. 'I hope you're ready for a challenge!'

Kieran nodded back eagerly. 'You bet, boss. Bring it on!'

First impressions were important. Kieran wanted to look confident, but not *too* confident. He was a young kid coming down from the Premier

League, and he needed to show respect towards Barnsley's experienced professionals. He wanted to learn from them; that's why he was there in the Championship.

However, Kieran also needed to prove himself at his new club. He didn't want the Barnsley players to think that he was a boy amongst men. He could handle himself! So, once the practice session started, he showed no fear. He wasn't the tallest or the strongest, but he was tough and he played with passion and belief.

'That's one way to introduce yourself to your new teammates!' Robins smiled to himself as Kieran won the ball with a crunching tackle. He sprinted down the right wing and delivered an incredible cross onto Daniel Bogdanović's head. *GOAL!*

The Barnsley manager was impressed, so impressed that he threw Kieran straight into the starting line-up, away at Middlesbrough. Within minutes, Kieran saved the day for his new team.

Boro's striker Chris Killen raced onto a long ball and flicked it past Barnsley's keeper, Luke Steele.

He looked up, expecting to find an open goal, but no, there was a defender in his way – Kieran! After sprinting back, he bravely blocked Killen's shot with his body.

'Thanks, Tripps!' Luke said, looking very relieved.

Sadly, Barnsley still lost the match, and shortly afterwards they lost at home to Plymouth Argyle too. It really wasn't the strong start that Kieran had hoped for. He was used to winning every week.

'Chin up, kid – you're doing a great job,' Robins reassured him. 'You couldn't have done anything about any of those goals.'

Kieran was desperate to win a game, or even a point, but it wasn't to be. In his third match for Barnsley, against Scunthorpe, he picked up an injury and, after just one month at his new club, that was the end. He returned to Manchester City, feeling a mix of pain and frustration.

'Unlucky, mate. You went to Barnsley and all you got was an injury!' Ben joked.

Kieran laughed it off and focused on getting fit again. After a few games for the Under-23s, he moved up to the City senior squad for their pre-season tour of the USA.

'Maybe Mancini hasn't forgotten about us, after all!' he told Ben, Andrew and Dedryck.

But despite Kieran's excitement, he didn't play a single minute of City's four matches in America. 'Why am I even here?' he wondered to himself. He was a footballer, not a tourist! He needed to get out and play. Surely, there was a club out there who actually wanted him?

Yes, Barnsley! Even in that short time in early 2010, Robins had spotted Kieran's amazing potential. He fought hard to get him back on loan for the whole of the next season, 2010–11.

'Thanks for believing in me, boss,' Kieran said to his manager. 'You won't regret it. This time, there'll be no stopping me!'

Every Championship game was a new and exciting challenge for Kieran. Some weeks, Kieran went toe to toe with tricky wingers like Wilfried Zaha at Crystal Palace and Scott Sinclair at Swansea City. Other weeks, he battled against big powerful forwards, and at other times, he had to close down dangerous crosses.

However, no-one in the league could deliver dangerous crosses quite like Kieran. That was his special talent, after all! In his first four games of the season, he set up three goals.

Against Bristol City, Kieran crossed the ball low and hard for Andy Gray to poke it in. GOAL!

Against Middlesbrough, he curled a corner-kick straight onto Jason Shackell's head. GOAL!

Against Norwich City, he swung in a free kick straight onto Jay McEveley's head. GOAL!

'Tripps, your right foot is ridiculous!' his grateful teammates cheered.

Kieran was delighted. All those hours on the City training ground with Jim and Steve had been totally worth it. He was part of the Barnsley team now.

Two wins and two clean sheets – this was the strong start that he had hoped for during his first loan spell. Second time around, he was playing game after game and really helping his team. Barnsley sat safely in mid-table, and Kieran's incredible crosses were making sure of that.

Against Nottingham Forest, he dribbled all the way to the by-line and then dragged the ball back with a clever Cruyff turn. When the left-back tried to tackle him, Kieran spun cleverly and chipped the ball to Andy at the back post. GOAL!

'Mate, you should be a winger with skills like that!' Jason shouted as they celebrated together.

Kieran shook his head, 'No thanks, it's much more fun to attack from the back!'

A few weeks later, Barnsley were losing 1–0 to Ipswich with seconds to go. Kieran needed to get the ball into the danger zone quickly before the referee blew the final whistle. His perfect pass reached Jacob Mellis just in time, who blasted the ball into the bottom corner. 1–1!

'Cheers, Tripps!' Jacob screamed, hugging him in front of the fans.

Everything was going so well for Kieran at Barnsley. With every game, he was improving. It still wasn't enough to impress Mancini at City, but it was enough to impress the England Under-21s manager,

Stuart Pearce. Kieran was called up for a friendly against Germany.

'Tripps!' his old Under-19 teammates Henri and Nathan cheered happily as the squad met up at the airport.

It was great to see his friends again, but Kieran was focused on football. He wanted to play and he wanted to shine. Unfortunately, it turned out to be a very difficult debut. The German winger Peniel Mlapa was big, strong and quick, and when he dribbled forward, it was so hard to stop him. Kieran lost the battle but he never gave up, and Pearce was pleased with his perseverance.

'Trippier had a solid game at right-back,' he told the media.

On his way back to Barnsley, Kieran beamed with pride. He was now only one step away from the England senior team, and one giant leap closer to his big World Cup dream.

CHAPTER 14

FREE-KICK WIZARD

It wasn't just Kieran's crossing skills that caught the eye at Barnsley; it was also his long-range shooting. When it came to free kicks, he could bend the ball like Beckham.

'You'd need two keepers to stop that!' Luke Steele complained as another strike flew into the top corner in training.

Kieran's homework was paying off. He still spent hours watching YouTube videos of Beckham and Italy's Andrea Pirlo. Their vision and technique were unbelievable! He never got tired of seeing the way they struck their free kicks and long passes. Perfection! Kieran tried to learn as much as he could from them and then put it into practice on the pitch.

Soon, Kieran was taking of all his team's set pieces. It was a big responsibility for a twenty-year-old, but he loved it. After creating lots of chances for others, surely it was only a matter of time before he scored one himself...

In February 2011, Barnsley were losing 3–2 against Leeds United – and there were just ten minutes to go. When Jacob won a free kick just outside the penalty area, Kieran rushed over to grab the ball first. He was determined to be the hero.

As he waited for the referee's whistle, Kieran thought about everything he had worked on with Steve at Manchester City. The run-up, the curl, the dip, the power. It was time to put it all together and score.

Usually, Kieran aimed his free kicks over the wall, or around it, but this time, the ball went *through* the wall. The Leeds keeper Kasper Schmeichel couldn't see a thing until it was too late. 3–3!

Goooooooooooooooooooooaaaaaaaaaaaaaaaaaallllllllllll llllllllllllllll!!!!!!!!!!!!!!!!!!!!

Kieran had scored his first senior goal, and in a Yorkshire derby too! He raced over to his manager, pumping his fists passionately.

'Get in!' he screamed at the centre of a big team hug.

It was the best feeling of his whole entire life. And after doing it once, Kieran was desperate to do it again.

In another Yorkshire derby – this time against Doncaster – he would get his chance. With five minutes to go, Barnsley were losing 2–1. Free kick! Stephen Foster ran forward to take it, but Kieran had a better idea.

'Trust me, I've got this!' he assured his teammate as he placed the ball down.

The tall wall jumped up but Kieran curled the ball over their heads and into the top corner. 2–2!

Gooooooooooooooooooooaaaaaaaaaaaaaaaallllllllllll llllllllllll!!!!!!!!!!!!!!!!

What a strike – Kieran to the rescue again! He ran over to the fans with his arms out wide for a hero's welcome. As a kid in Bury, he had dreamt about moments like this. Now, it was really happening to him.

'You're a legend!' his fans and teammates screamed.

Kieran was loving life at Barnsley but as the games flew by, his return to Manchester City got closer and closer. He had learnt so much during his first full season of senior football. He didn't want it to end.

What a season it had been – forty-one games, eight clean sheets, six assists, two goals, and the Barnsley Young Player of the Year award. Kieran was really going to miss everyone at the club and they were going to miss him too.

'Come back next year, Tripps!' the supporters begged.

'How am I meant to score goals without you?' Andy joked as they said their goodbyes.

'It's been an absolute pleasure working with you,' Robins told him. 'You're going to be a top, top player one of these days!'

It was a sad and confusing time for Kieran. When Barnsley tried to buy him, Manchester City said no.

Okay, so did that mean that they were going to give him a chance?

It didn't seem that way, though, because a few weeks later, he was sent out on loan again!

Burnley really needed a new right-back, and Kieran was top of Eddie Howe's wish-list. The manager wanted his team to play fast, attacking football and that suited his style perfectly.

'Let's do this!' Kieran agreed immediately.

Burnley were still a Championship side, but hopefully not for much longer. They were chasing promotion, rather than battling relegation. Kieran had played with Jay Rodriguez at Barnsley, and he knew that he was a top striker. It also helped that his friend Ben was already there at Burnley. Together, they would get The Clarets back into the Premier League.

'We're going to show City what they're missing!' they cheered.

Against Cardiff City, Kieran dribbled forward and then *ZOOM!* With a clever stepover, he beat the left-back, and kept on running. What next? Even at top speed, he still delivered a perfect cross for Charlie Austin to head home. *GOAL!*

'Nice one, Tripps!' Ben shouted from defence.

Kieran had his first Burnley assist, but what about his first Burnley goal? It was a free kick, of course! In the League Cup against Milton Keynes Dons, he curled the ball up over the wall and it dipped down into the bottom corner.

Gooooooooooooooooooooaaaaaaaaaaaaaaaalllllllllllll llllllllllllll!!!!!!!!!!!!!!!!!!!!

Kieran lept up and punched the air. He was off the mark at Burnley! New club, same free-kick king.

CHAPTER 15

LEAVING CITY BEHIND

It was 0–0, with thirty minutes gone. As the ball came to Kieran on the edge of the Brighton penalty area, he took a quick touch to control it and then *BANG!* His shot flew through a crowd of defenders, past the goalkeeper, and into the top corner.

*Goooooooooooooooooooooaaaaaaaaaaaaaaaaalllllllllllll
lllllllllllll!!!!!!!!!!!!!!!!!!*

Kieran was having so much fun at Burnley that he almost forgot about Manchester City. He still checked their results every weekend, and messaged Jim and Steve, but he no longer felt part of his childhood club. He was a Claret now.

So, Kieran was delighted when Eddie Howe told

him that he wanted to sign him permanently.

'I know your loan deal lasts until the end of the season but we want to buy you now,' the Burnley manager explained. 'You're a huge part of this team and you're getting better and better. We really don't want to lose you in the summer!'

Kieran was desperate to keep playing week in week out. Howe was right about him; he was improving all the time. Burnley were a big club. They had been in the Premier League before, and they were trying to get back there as quickly as possible.

That fitted perfectly with Kieran's plans. He was determined to work his way back up to the top, but would City let him leave? Yes, they would. After thirteen years at the club, Kieran was finally saying goodbye for good.

'Are you sure this is what you want?' Jim asked him before he signed his contract.

Kieran shrugged, 'City are never going to give me a chance. I'm twenty-one now – it's time for me to move on with my career.'

'I know, I know, but they're making a massive

mistake with you! Good luck, kid. Go and become a superstar and prove them wrong.'

A week later, Ben also signed for Burnley. Together, both friends were leaving City behind.

'No regrets,' they agreed.

Their new club certainly had no regrets. For £400,000, Kieran was an absolute bargain for Burnley. He scored a screamer against Middlesbrough from forty yards out, and then set up two goals for Jay against Nottingham Forest.

'I'm so glad you're staying!' the striker cried out as they celebrated.

However, Kieran's dream of playing in the Premier League would have to wait another year. Burnley finished the 2011–12 season only thirteenth in the Championship. It had been a disappointing season for the team, but not for their right-back – after starring in all forty-six league matches, Kieran won the Burnley Player of the Year award.

'And I'm only just getting started!' he told his teammates happily.

Kieran couldn't wait for the 2012–13 season to

begin. For the first time in years, he felt settled. Burnley was a great club and he believed they were good enough to get back into the Premier League. Yes, Jay had now just signed for Southampton, but they had been joined by Danny Ings, who was up front with Charlie. One day soon, Kieran would return to the Etihad to play *against* Manchester City.

That idea really spurred Kieran on. He raced down the Burnley right, delivering incredible crosses all game long. Against Sheffield Wednesday, he got a hat-trick – a hat-trick of assists!

On the run, Kieran swung a dangerous ball into the six-yard box. Charlie outjumped the centre-back and... *GOAL!*

Despite being a defender, Kieran was now Burnley's danger man. Every time his teammates got the ball, they looked to pass to him.

'Cross it in, Tripps!' the fans encouraged him.

The team relied on his remarkable right foot. Kieran picked out Charlie again, this time at the back post. His diving header flew past the Wednesday keeper. *GOAL!*

Burnley's deadly duo saved their best goal for last. Kieran got the ball in his own half and played a perfect long pass up to Charlie. He beat the defender and fired the ball into the back of the net. *GOAL!*

'You guys are on fire!' Ben cheered.

But Burnley's wonderful hat-trick still wasn't enough to win the game against Wednesday – it ended in a 3–3 draw. What was going on? They were awesome in attack, but really bad at the back.

That had to change. When Sean Dyche became the new Burnley manager, his first task was to tighten up the defence.

'Uh-oh,' Kieran thought to himself. 'Does that mean I won't be able to get forward anymore?'

But instead of asking him to change his style, Dyche just asked him to improve his defending.

'You're the best crosser in the Championship,' Kieran's new manager told him, 'but it's no good setting up one goal, and then giving another goal away. We're going to turn you into the complete right-back.'

The complete right-back? Kieran loved the sound

of that. He was going to work as hard as possible to become 'The New Gary Neville'. That was his dream.

With practice, practice, practice, the Burnley back four became a much stronger unit. Kieran got better at keeping the opposition left wingers quiet. He marked them tightly, he tracked their runs and he blocked their crosses.

'That's it, Tripps!' Dyche clapped and cheered on the sidelines. 'Great defending!'

Then when he got the chance to attack, *ZOOM!* Kieran raced down the right to deliver more of his incredible crosses for Charlie and Danny to score. He finished the season with twelve assists, the third-highest in the whole league.

'Not bad for a defender!' Dyche said with a smile. He was proud of Kieran's progress.

It had been another disappointing year for Burnley, but another amazing year for their star right-back. This time, Kieran was even named in the Championship Team of the Year.

'Next year, we'll all be in there,' he told the other

Burnley players confidently. 'We're going up, lads – I know it!'

Kieran's old England Under-19 teammate, Kyle Walker, had won the Premier League's Young Player of the Year award at Tottenham. Kieran reasoned that if 'Walks' could do it, then so could he! One more season in the Championship, and Kieran would be 100 per cent ready to take on the top division too.

CHAPTER 16

GOING UP!

Thanks to Dyche's help, Kieran was now the most complete and consistent right-back in the whole of the Championship. He was hard to beat at the back, and impossible to stop in attack.

In August 2013, in another game against Sheffield Wednesday, Kieran dribbled past the opposition's defender, and whipped in another brilliant cross to the back post. 2–0 to Burnley!

'What a ball, Tripps!' cheered the goalscorer, Sam Vokes.

With Charlie now at QPR, Sam and Danny were Burnley's new star strikeforce. They were having the time of their lives, thanks to Kieran's incredible crosses.

He wasn't the only one creating chances, though. The Clarets had Junior Stanislas and Ross Wallace on the wings, and new signings David Jones, Dean Marney and Scott Arfield in the middle. It was a real team effort and by November, Burnley were top of the table. Kieran was on track to achieve his Premier League dream.

'Well done, lads. We've got to keep this up now!' Dyche urged his players.

Second-place would be enough to get Burnley back into the Premier League, but Kieran was desperate to win the Championship title. He really wanted his first trophy in senior football. Manchester City's FA Youth Cup triumph felt like a very long time ago, and he had been too injured at the time to even enjoy it properly.

'Come on, this is our year!' he shouted.

Kieran was still only twenty-three, but after playing over 150 matches, he now felt like an experienced pro. He was a strong character and he was one of the team leaders, in the dressing room and out on the pitch. When they needed him most, he always delivered.

Against his old club, Barnsley, in December 2013, Kieran battled his way down the wing before finding Michael Kightly in space. 1–0 to Burnley!

Against their promotion rivals, Leicester City, a week later, he pinged it through the penalty area to Danny. 1–1!

Kieran was having another sensational season. He celebrated the New Year in style by scoring the winner against Huddersfield Town.

With ten minutes to go, Dean chipped a long-ball forward, aiming for one of the Burnley strikers. But instead, it was Kieran who burst into the box and dribbled around the keeper.

'Go on, Tripps!' the supporters shouted out in shock.

Except for another fantastic free kick in the League Cup, Kieran hadn't scored a goal for nearly two years. Was this his big moment? The angle was tight but somehow, he stretched out his right leg and fired the ball in off the crossbar.

Goooooooooooooooooooaaaaaaaaaaaaaaaallllllllllll llllllllllllll!!!!!!!!!!!!!!!!!!

As he ran towards the corner, Kieran blew kisses to all the fans. 'We're going up!' he called out confidently. Hadn't he said that all along?

With each hard-fought victory, The Clarets got closer and closer to promotion. It was Leicester who won the Championship title, but after a 2–0 home win over Wigan Athletic, Burnley joined them in the Premier League.

Hurrrraaaaaaaaaaaaaaayyyyy!!

The scenes at the final whistle were unforgettable. Thousands of happy fans stormed onto the Turf Moor pitch to celebrate with their heroes.

'Nice one, Tripps, you legend!'

We love you Burnley, we do,
We love you Burnley, we do,
We love you Burnley, we do,
Oh Burnley we love you!

Later on, in the dressing room, there was champagne flying everywhere as the players hugged and chanted:

We are going up, say we are going up!!
We are going up, say we are going up!!

It was by far the best moment of Kieran's career.
He had always believed in himself, and in his
teammates. As they stood there, arm in arm, a feeling
of pure joy buzzed all the way through his body.
What an achievement! Together, they had done it;
they had led Burnley back into the Premier League.

'Aren't you glad we left City behind?' Kieran
asked Ben.

His friend just laughed. 'What? City who?'

Kieran's season soon got even better. He finished
top of the assists chart, with twelve, and made
the Championship Team of the Year for a second
time in a row. He was proud of himself, but most
of all, he was proud of his team. Burnley had only
conceded thirty-seven goals all season. That was the
lowest in the league! The defence said a big thank
you to Dyche.

'We couldn't have done this without you, Boss!'

Kieran couldn't wait for his next big challenge
to begin. He was ready to take on the best clubs in
England – Manchester United, Chelsea, Liverpool,
Arsenal, Tottenham, and of course, his old club

Manchester City. It hadn't been easy, but Kieran had battled his way back to the highest level.

'Bring it on!'

Over the summer of 2014, there were rumours that Arsenal wanted to sign him, but Kieran ignored them and signed a new contract at Burnley. He was happy and settled at Turf Moor. This was the club that had shown faith in him, and so this was the club that he would play for in his first Premier League adventure.

CHAPTER 17

GOING DOWN

Kieran couldn't have asked for a tougher Premier League debut. Burnley were playing Chelsea, and that meant that he was up against their Belgian wing wizard, Eden Hazard.

'Bring it on!' he shouted in the dressing room before kick-off.

Dyche had signed a few new players but mostly, he was sticking with his stars from the Championship. They deserved their chance at the top level.

When Scott scored a great goal to put Burnley 1–0 up, Turf Moor went wild. What a start!

'Get in!' Kieran roared in front of the fans.

Unfortunately, their lead didn't last long. Kieran kept Hazard quiet when he was out on the left, but the playmaker moved all over the pitch. Plus, Chelsea had Diego Costa, Oscar and Cesc Fàbregas too. Twenty minutes later, Burnley were 3–1 down.

'We can't give them free headers like that!' Kieran groaned, throwing his arms up in frustration.

They were playing at the top level now, against awesome attackers who only needed one chance to score. Burnley didn't have time to slowly find their feet in the Premier League. They needed to improve their defending immediately, and so that's exactly what they did.

They drew 0–0 against Manchester United...

Then 0–0 against Crystal Palace...

And then 0–0 against Sunderland too!

The Clarets had won their first points of the season, but they'd only scored one goal in six games! Danny was crying out for Kieran's incredible crosses, but he was too busy at the back.

In the Manchester United game, Ashley Young attacked down the left wing but Kieran won the ball off him. As Wayne Rooney ran in for the tackle, he flicked it through his legs. Nutmeg!

'Nice one, Tripps!' the Burnley fans cheered.

Kieran was loving every minute of life in the Premier League. Game after game, he was battling against quality wingers, and every single one was different. Palace's Wilfried Zaha was a deadly dribbler, whereas West Brom's Chris Brunt liked to cross the ball with his lethal left-foot. And Arsenal's Alexis Sánchez? Well, he was amazing at everything.

After ten games, Burnley languished at the bottom of the table, with six defeats, four draws, and ZERO wins. Some people were saying that they were the worst Premier League team EVER.

'Come on, let's prove them wrong today!' Dyche told his players before their eleventh game, a big home match against Hull City.

Kieran was determined to win the three points for his team. In the fiftieth minute, the ball bounced out to him on the right wing. He was in lots of space, so he took his time. He controlled it, looked up, and then calmly curled it into the box. As soon as it left his boot, Kieran knew that it was one of his incredible crosses.

Power? Perfect!

Direction? The danger zone!

All it needed was a striker's touch to turn it into a goal. The ball flew over Danny's head, then George Boyd's, but Ashley Barnes was there at the back post to flick it over the goalkeeper's arms. 1–0!

Ashley punched the air and ran over to thank Kieran. 'What a ball!' he cried out.

For the next forty minutes, the Burnley defenders stood strong like soldiers. Tackle! Block! Header! Interception! When the final whistle blew, the players celebrated as if they had just won the league.

'We are staying up, say we are staying up!'

It wouldn't be easy but Burnley believed.

At last, it was time for the match that Kieran and Ben had been waiting for – away at Manchester City! It felt very strange returning to the Etihad Stadium to play for another team. There were so many memories and familiar faces.

'Look who it is!' Jim called out when he spotted Kieran. 'Are you here for revenge?'

'Hopefully!'

The two clubs were at opposite ends of the league. City were in second place and challenging for the title, while Burnley were nineteenth and fighting relegation.

At half-time, City were 2–0 up and cruising. David Silva and Jesús Navas were making Ben's life a misery on the left. But after Dyche's team-talk, Burnley came out battling. The game wasn't over yet.

George steered Danny's cross past Joe Hart. 2–1!

Then, with ten minutes to go, Ashley fired a shot into the top corner. 2–2!

'Get in!' Kieran screamed as the players hugged in front of their fans. He was so proud of all his teammates. They stuck together and never gave up, no matter what.

Burnley held on for a famous draw against the richest club in the world. For Kieran, it was one of many magical moments in his first Premier

League season. There were no fantastic free kicks, but there was:

A deep, curling corner-kick against Crystal Palace, which Ben headed home at the back post.

A bursting run down the right at Old Trafford, which ended with a teasing cross and Danny's diving header.

And another Kieran and Ben double act at Stamford Bridge. Six years after playing there for Manchester City in the FA Youth Cup Final, they earned a late point for Burnley.

Sadly, not even these high points were enough to keep them up. Despite another 1–0 win over Hull City, they were relegated back to the Championship. A year after going up, Burnley were going down again.

'Well done lads, I'm proud of you all,' Dyche told his disappointed team in the dressing room. 'We've learned a lot this season and we have to keep moving forward. We gave it our best shot and we'll be back.'

Kieran had always known that it would be a difficult season but he couldn't help feeling devastated. It was gutting after all that hard work.

He had played in all thirty-eight Premier League matches, and he believed that he was good enough to stay.

After the final home match at Turf Moor, Kieran walked around the pitch with Danny, clapping their loyal fans.

'Please don't leave!' the supporters shouted back at them.

Kieran and Danny had been Burnley's star players all season, and top clubs like Liverpool and Tottenham now wanted to buy them. They really didn't want to leave the club, but they also really didn't want to leave the Premier League behind.

Over that summer, Kieran would have a difficult decision to make.

CHAPTER 18

TO TOTTENHAM

'I'd like to thank everyone involved at Burnley for four memorable years,' Kieran tweeted. 'A great club with great fans.'

He didn't leave it at that, though. He felt that he owed the fans a proper explanation. 'I was devastated when we got relegated because I didn't want to leave the club. But I want to play in the Premier League and be the best player I can be.'

The Burnley supporters were sad to see Kieran leave but they understood. He wasn't such a young player anymore. He was twenty-four now, and he had to do what was best for his career.

Plus, it was hard to say no to a top club like

Tottenham. Their manager, Mauricio Pochettino, was building a brilliant team, packed with young England internationals. They had Harry Kane, Dele Alli, Eric Dier, Danny Rose and, of course, his old Under-19 teammate, Kyle Walker.

'Won't you and Walks be playing the same position?' Ben asked Kieran.

Ben was clearly desperate for Kieran to stay at Burnley, but it was still a good question. Kyle was a right-back too, and one of the best in the Premier League. Would Kieran be joining Spurs just to sit on the bench?

'No, you'll get plenty of opportunities,' Pochettino promised him. 'We're going to have a lot of matches next season, in the Premier League, the League Cup, the FA Cup, *and* the Europa League. We believe that you can really improve our squad. You'll have to fight for your place but so will everyone else.'

Kieran nodded eagerly. He was ready to fight for his place at Spurs, and to learn from Kyle too. After all, he would be making a big step-up from Burnley. There would be no more relegation battles. Instead,

Tottenham would be battling against Chelsea, Liverpool, Manchester United and his old club Manchester City for a Champions League spot.

If he signed for Spurs, Kieran could soon be playing against the likes of Barcelona and Real Madrid. And fingers crossed, he could be playing for England too.

'What do you think I should do?' he asked Kelvin. Even now that Kieran was a Premier League player, he still always asked his big brother for advice.

'You've got to go for it, bro!' Kelvin replied. 'They're one of the biggest clubs in Europe!'

Good – that was exactly what Kieran wanted to hear. He was making the right decision by signing for Spurs. He just had to believe in his own ability.

'I can do this!' he told himself.

Firstly, however, he needed to say a sad goodbye to everyone at Burnley. It was an emotional day, full of hugs, laughs and best wishes:

'Good luck, Tripps! Hopefully, we'll get to play you in the cup this season!'

'And then twice next season once we're back in the Premier League!'

Kieran was really going to miss his teammates, especially his best friends Ben and Danny. He was really going to miss his manager too.

'Thanks for everything, boss,' Kieran said. 'Without you, I wouldn't be half the defender that I am now!'

Dyche smiled. 'Yes, I like to think I've taught you a thing or two! But seriously, you've worked really hard for this chance, Tripps. You're a top Premier League player, so go to Tottenham and show it.'

For £3.5 million, Kieran became Spurs' cheapest signing of the summer. He wasn't exactly the big-name buy that some fans were hoping for. 'Kieran who?' some people asked, but he didn't mind that. He would just have to make sure that they remembered his name.

Wearing a smart white shirt, Kieran posed for photos next to the big club badge at White Hart Lane. In his hands, he held up the brand-new Tottenham home kit. What number would he choose? Kyle already had the Number 2 shirt...

'What else is available?' Kieran asked. He was happy to wear whatever he was given.

'9?'

'No sorry, I can't wear 9 – I'm a right-back!'

'What about 16?'

'Yes, that's fine, thanks!' he replied. He had worn that number at Barnsley all those years ago.

Kieran couldn't wait to get started. He had so many talented new teammates to meet! As well as their England stars, Tottenham also had Christian Eriksen, Jan Vertonghen, Mousa Dembélé, Son Heung-min… Their list of stars went on and on.

Kieran had played against most of them for Burnley but playing *with* them was a different and daunting idea. What if he wasn't good enough? What if he couldn't compete? Luckily, when he arrived for his first day of pre-season training, his old friend Kyle was there to greet him with a big hug.

'Mate, it's great to have you here,' he said. 'Tottenham's definitely big enough for the both of us.'

Once the session started, however, Kyle put his game-face on. They weren't friends anymore; they were two rivals, challenging for Spurs' one right-back spot.

'Right, Tripps, let the battle begin!'

CHAPTER 19

FIGHTING FIT

Kieran was on the Tottenham bench for the first match of the 2015–16 Premier League season against Manchester United at Old Trafford. The manager had warned him that Kyle would be starting at right-back instead, but it was still frustrating not to play – at Burnley, Kieran had only missed six league matches in four whole years.

'Just be patient,' he told himself. Pochettino had promised that he would get chances.

Memphis Depay attacked down the right for United and crossed the ball to Wayne Rooney, who had ample space in the penalty area. Where was Kyle? He was sprinting back from the halfway line!

Kyle got there just in time to tackle Rooney but his touch took the ball past Hugo Lloris and into the net. *Own goal!*

Tottenham lost the match 1–0.

'Bring in Trippier!' some fans cried out at the final whistle but Pochettino stuck with Kyle instead. Kieran was disappointed and desperate to make his debut. Why was he still on the bench?

'We need to get you fit first,' his manager explained.

Kieran had arrived at his new club after a relaxing holiday in Mexico. Yes, he was a little heavier and slower than usual, but wasn't that what pre-season training was for? No – not at a top team like Tottenham; Pochettino expected his players to be fighting fit all the time.

'You're an elite athlete,' the manager told Kieran, 'so you have to be dedicated and professional.'

Kieran learnt his lesson. Pochettino expected a really high standard from his players, so he couldn't switch off for a second. If he did, he would be dropped straight away. With extra training and a better diet, Kieran soon felt fitter than ever. All he needed now was a chance to impress.

At first, Kieran's chances all came in the Europa League. He played every minute of every match in the competition, and he enjoyed his first taste of European football. Tottenham finished top of Group J, after beating big clubs like Anderlecht and Monaco.

'Come on, we can win the whole tournament!' Kieran cried out as the team celebrated yet another goal at White Hart Lane.

The tactics really suited his style. Pochettino pushed his full-backs really far forward – Kieran on the right, and Ben Davies on the left. They were a key part of Spurs' exciting European attack, alongside Son Heung-min, Nacer Chadli and Érik Lamela.

In the Premier League, however, Kieran was still waiting for his first Tottenham start. Would it ever come? Yes, just after Christmas, Pochettino finally decided to rest Kyle against Watford. Kieran was in!

'Right, I have to make the most of this,' he told himself.

Tottenham took an early lead at Vicarage Road but

with time running out, the game was tied at 1–1. Spurs were in danger of dropping down to fifth place. Unless...

The ball came out to Kieran on the right. Could he deliver one of his incredible crosses? His first attempt was blocked but he got a second chance. This time, he picked out Son, who flicked the ball cleverly past the keeper. 2–1!

As the Spurs fans danced with joy, Son ran straight over to celebrate with Kieran.

'What a goal!'

'What a cross!'

Kieran was delighted to be one of Tottenham's heroes. Would he get to keep his place after saving the day? No – Pochettino brought Kyle back for the next game against Everton, but he did give Kieran more and more opportunities: a game against Sunderland, then Crystal Palace and then the return match against Watford.

Kieran had really missed playing week in week out in the Premier League. Although the European adventures were fun, the crowds weren't as big and the atmosphere just wasn't the same. But for a three o'clock kick-off on a Saturday, White Hart Lane was full of fans and full of singing.

Come on you Spurs!

We love you Tottenham, we do!

In the first half of that return match against Watford, Ben dribbled into the Watford penalty area twice, but both of his shots were saved by the keeper.

In the second half, it was Kieran's turn to attack. He curled a teasing cross towards Nacer but a Watford defender cleared it just in time.

'So close!' Kieran groaned, looking up at the sky.

Tottenham needed to find a winning goal from somewhere, but where? As Dele attacked down the left wing, Kieran sprinted forward down the right.

'Cross it!' he called out with his arm up in the air.

Dele passed the ball all the way to the back post, to give Kieran a simple tap-in. 1–0!

Goooooooooooooooooooaaaaaaaaaaaaaaaallllllllllll lllllllllllllll!!!!!!!!!!!!!!!!!!!!

What a moment! It was Kieran's first-ever

Tottenham goal. As he ran towards the corner flag, he jumped up and punched the air.

'Get in!' he cheered.

Now the fans would definitely remember Kieran's name because that goal turned out to be the matchwinner. Spurs stayed in second place in the table, just five points behind Leicester City.

Was Kieran about to become a Premier League champion? He didn't have time to think about that – he had another Europa League match to win. When Nacer got the ball on the right wing, Kieran raced forward on an overlapping run.

'Yes!' he called out for the pass.

Kieran's delivery was so deadly that the Fiorentina defender scored an own goal. 3–0!

His teammates rushed over to congratulate Kieran on his cross.

'That's your goal really!' Nacer told him.

Unfortunately, Spurs ended their excellent season without winning a single trophy. Borussia Dortmund knocked them out of the Europa League, and Leicester held on to clinch the Premier League title.

'Next year, we'll be unstoppable!' Pochettino reassured his players.

Kieran was satisfied with his first season at Tottenham – nineteen games, three assists and one goal. It was a decent start, and there was plenty more to come. The Spurs supporters hadn't seen him at his absolute best yet.

'You better watch out!' he joked with Kyle. Their friendly rivalry was pushing them both to get better and better.

Kieran wasn't getting as much game-time as he had at Burnley, but he didn't even think about leaving. He couldn't give up after one year. He had to stay and fight for his place. During the summer, Southampton tried to sign him, but Pochettino said no.

Phew! Kieran was happy at the club, especially now that Tottenham were playing in the Champions League. They would need their two talented right-backs more than ever.

CHAPTER 30

BREAKING THROUGH

Despite Kieran's positivity, the first half of the next
season was almost exactly the same as the last.
Again, Kyle was Tottenham's Premier League right-
back and again, Kieran only played in Europe and
the League Cup.

'Your chance will come,' Pochettino kept
promising Kieran, but the player needed to know
when. He couldn't wait forever. And who were
Spurs' opponents when Kieran finally started another
league match? Watford again!

There was one important difference, though – his
position. Instead of playing on the right of a back
four, he was now playing as the right wing-back,
ahead of a back three.

'Great!' Kieran thought to himself. 'Now, I can attack even more!'

This was his big opportunity to shine after weeks on the sidelines. He had hardly played since Tottenham's 2–1 defeat to Monaco in the Champions League. Was Pochettino punishing him for one poor performance? It didn't matter. There was only way for Kieran to prove himself – by assisting Spurs to victory.

Harry Kane was excited to have Kieran back in the team. As a striker, it was so much fun playing with such an incredible crosser. Kieran didn't let him, or his team, down. He looked up and slipped a perfect pass into Harry's path. All Harry had to do was shoot...1–0!

Harry ran towards his teammate with a big smile on his face. 'Cheers Tripps, I knew you'd set me up today!'

Five minutes later, Kieran did it again. He controlled Dele's pass and curled the ball straight into the danger zone. He knew exactly where Harry wanted it. 2–0 – game over!

'What a cross, mate!' he shouted, hugging Kieran tightly. 'I wish we could play you and Walks in the same team. I would never stop scoring!'

Kieran wished that too. When he played, Tottenham almost always won. Why couldn't he play together with Kyle? Surely, it didn't have to be one or the other – it could be both!

'Think of all the double trouble we could cause!' Kieran thought to himself. Still, two assists on 1 January felt like a very good sign.

'2017 is going to be my year!' Kieran told himself confidently.

In fact, his big Tottenham breakthrough was only a few months away. From March until the end of that season, Kieran became a Premier League regular again.

He wasn't surprised when Pochettino picked him to play against his old club Burnley; Kyle needed a rest after two tiring matches for England.

Kieran wasn't surprised when he started against Watford either. It felt like he always playing against them! In the second half, he crossed and Son scored. 4–0!

The shock only came when Kieran kept his place against Arsenal. The North London Derby? Surely, Pochettino would pick Kyle for that! But no, it was definitely Kieran's name written there in the starting line-up – '16 TRIPPIER'. At last, he was breaking through.

'Congratulations, you deserve this,' his dad Chris told him. 'Just make sure you take this opportunity!'

For eighty minutes, Kieran ran up and down the right wing tirelessly for Tottenham. He did his duties brilliantly, both in defence and attack. When he came off for Kyle, they were 2–0 up and the White Hart Lane crowd gave him a loud standing ovation.

'Well played!' Pochettino said, giving him a quick hug on the touchline.

Kieran was buzzing as he sat down on the Spurs bench. What a win it would be, especially against their London rivals! It would leave them only four points behind Chelsea at the top of the table, with four games to go. Could Tottenham win the Premier League title this time?

Despite Kieran's best efforts, though, the answer

was no. He helped his team to beat Manchester
· United but by then it was too late. In the one match
he missed, Spurs lost 1–0 to West Ham.

'Not again!' the fans groaned.

It was the same old story for Spurs, but not for
Kieran. He was no longer their second-choice right-
back. All that hard work and patience was finally
paying off. He had fought his way into the Tottenham
team.

Kieran saved his best performance of the season for
the final game against Hull City. Harry was desperate
to win the Premier League Golden Boot for the second
year in a row, and he needed Kieran's help.

'Come on, Tripps,' he shouted in the dressing
room. 'With your crosses, I can definitely get a hat-
trick today!'

As Eric dribbled the ball forward, Kieran made his
move into the penalty area. The pass was perfect, so
perfect that Kieran decided to cross it first-time on
the volley. He was playing with lots of confidence. As
always, Harry was in the right place at the right time
to finish things off. 2–0!

Their understanding was unbelievable. It was like they had been playing together forever.

'Thanks, I knew I could rely on you!' Harry said, putting an arm around his teammate.

Kieran smiled. 'Next season, I'll make sure you score even more, H!'

It wasn't just Harry that he was helping, though, in the Hull game. In the second half, he set up Toby Alderweireld to make it 7–1. What a way for Kieran to end his breakthrough season at Spurs.

Soon, the right-back role would be Kieran's to keep, as Kyle moved to Manchester City for £50million.

'Good luck, Walks. Thanks for everything!'

'Good luck, Tripps! That Number 2 shirt is yours now!'

It was far from the end of their rivalry, though. Instead of competing against each other at Tottenham, they would now be competing against each other in the Premier League, and also for England.

CHAPTER 21

ENGLAND CALL-UP

A few days after Spurs' 7–1 thrashing of Hull, Kieran was told that Pochettino wanted to see him in his office. His first reaction was panic. Was he in trouble? Had he done something wrong? He couldn't think of anything...

As Kieran walked in and shut the door behind him, his heart was pounding in his chest. He glanced up at his manager but his face wasn't giving anything away.

'I know what you did last night,' Pochettino said at last.

Last night? Kieran tried to think clearly. Where had he been? He had been at home with his wife,

Charlotte, looking after their baby son, Jacob, all night.

'Boss, I—' he began to say but Pochettino was already on the phone.

'Hi Hugo, could you come to my office please?'

Uh-oh! Hugo Lloris was the Tottenham captain. He looked very serious as he entered the room. Kieran had a horrible feeling in the pit of his stomach. What had he done?

Suddenly, a smile spread across Pochettino's face. 'Congratulations, you've been called up to the England squad!'

'Well done, Tripps!' Hugo added.

Kieran didn't know whether to laugh or cry. He had never given up hope of representing his country at senior level. Even when his last Under-21 cap had become a distant memory, he had refused to believe that his England career was over. He was right all along!

After thanking his manager and captain, Kieran walked out into the corridor. He had a phone call to make.

'Mum, Dad,' he said. 'I've been called up to the England squad!'

There was a brief pause on the other end of the line, followed by shrieks of joy.

'Son, that's brilliant news!' Chris shouted.

'We're so proud of you!' Eleanor told him tearfully.

'I really couldn't have done it without you guys,' Kieran replied. He was feeling emotional too. 'Thanks for everything – I owe you!'

'We'll start booking our tickets!'

'No, leave everything to me, Dad. I'll sort it out!'

Kieran thought back to his childhood, and all those hours sat by his dad's side, supporting the national team. Chris was England's biggest fan. During the 2010 World Cup, he had even flown a giant St George's flag outside their home in Bury. The local council asked him to take it down but Chris refused. Now his son was about to play for England! It didn't get any better than that.

Kieran was the only new name in the squad for the matches against Scotland and France. It was a little daunting at first, but at least he was surrounded by familiar faces. He knew the goalkeeper Tom Heaton from Burnley, and four of his Tottenham teammates were there too: Harry, Dele, Eric and Kyle.

'I wish you'd stop following me around, Tripps!' Kyle joked.

Kieran was on the bench for the first match in May 2017 – the World Cup qualifier against Scotland at Hampden Park. England needed to win and so their manager Gareth Southgate picked his strongest team. That meant Harry up front, Dele in midfield and Kyle at right-back.

'Come on, England!' Kieran cheered along with the rest of the fans.

But with seconds to go, they were losing 2–1. What a disaster! On the subs bench, Kieran couldn't sit still. He wanted to be out there so badly, crossing the ball in for Harry to score. Instead, it was Raheem Sterling who set Harry up. 2–2!

'Get in!' Kieran shouted, jumping out of his seat to celebrate.

Three days later, England played their second match – a friendly against France. This time,

Southgate decided to try something new. He went for a back three with wing-backs, just like Pochettino at Tottenham. And just like at Tottenham, Kieran would be playing on the right!

He had a quick phone call to make:

'Dad, I'm starting tonight!'

'That's great, son! We'll be there cheering you on in the crowd. See you later!'

Kieran had to take lots of deep breaths as he walked out of the tunnel onto the pitch in Paris. The atmosphere in the Stade de France was amazing, as 75,000 people sang Oasis's 'Don't Look Back in Anger' at the tops of their voices. The England fans held up pieces of white and red paper to form a giant St George's flag. It was even bigger than the one his dad had put up back home in Bury.

As the anthems played, Kieran stood there dressed in all-white, except for the three blue lions on his shirt. He was an England international now, and it was the proudest moment of his entire life.

Five years earlier, Kieran had left Manchester City behind to battle his way up from the Championship

– and look at him now! But there was no time to
stop and enjoy the moment. Kieran had a match
to win.

England got off to a dream start. Dele passed
to Raheem, who flicked it to Ryan Bertrand. Ryan
crossed to Harry. 1–0!

Right, time to focus. On the right, Kieran stayed
calm and kept things simple. He didn't want to make
any mistakes on his debut. By half-time, however, it
was 2–1 to France. Their young stars Kylian Mbappé,
Ousmane Dembélé and Paul Pogba were teaching
England a tough lesson.

'Welcome to international football!' Kieran thought
to himself as he picked himself up and carried on. He
still had a lot to learn at the highest level.

After seventy-six minutes, with the score at 2–2,
Kieran was substituted. It was a solid start to his
international career and as he left the field, he hoped
that he had done enough to get another England
chance.

'Well done!' Southgate said, patting him on the
back.

'Well done!' his mum shouted too when they met up after the match. In the end, England had lost 3–2 but Kieran wasn't letting anything ruin his big day.

'I've never cried so much in my life!' his dad admitted. 'You played really well, son.'

Well enough to get another England call-up? Kieran would have to wait and see. The 2018 World Cup was now only one year away. If he had a strong season as Tottenham's first-choice right-back, who knew what might happen...

CHAPTER 22

FIRST-CHOICE, FINALLY!

Tottenham had a new 'Number 2' for the 2017–18 season: Kieran! He had certainly earned the shirt. After waiting patiently for his chance, he was finally first-choice.

He wasn't Spurs' only option at right-back, though. Pochettino had replaced Kyle with Serge Aurier from PSG. Although Serge cost a lot of money, that didn't worry Kieran. He was focused on his own game and he wasn't giving up his starting spot without a real fight.

'Are you ready, Tripps?' Harry shouted eagerly as the season kicked off. He couldn't wait to carry on their perfect partnership.

Kieran nodded eagerly. 'Let's go out there and score some goals!'

Over the summer, he had been working hard on his attacking play. As a wing-back, Kieran couldn't just cross the ball every time. That was too predictable and too easy for the defenders. He had to find other ways of getting the ball forward to Dele and Harry – short passes, long passes, through-balls.

'I've got a full box of tricks now,' he told his brother, Kelvin. 'Just you wait and see!'

In the Premier League against Everton, Kieran passed to Harry and kept running down the right for the one-two. But Harry decided to whip the ball into the box instead. It flew over everyone's head, including the keeper. *GOAL!*

'Was that a cross or a shot?' Kieran asked as they celebrated together.

Harry smiled and shrugged. 'Does it matter? I scored!'

In the Champions League against APOEL Nicosia, the one-two worked brilliantly. Harry passed it wide to Kieran and then burst into the box, calling for one of his incredible crosses. One touch, a quick look up, and then BANG! Kieran made it look so easy, as he curled the ball straight onto Harry's head. *GOAL!*

'Tripps, what would I do without you?' he screamed, hugging him tightly. With Kieran's help, Harry had his first hat-trick of the season.

Against Huddersfield, Kieran set him up with a header. Tottenham's Number 10 chased after it and fired a shot into the bottom corner. *GOAL!*

'Cheers, mate!' Harry cheered, giving him a high-five.

Fifteen minutes later, Kieran threw the ball to Harry and he turned and scored. *GOAL!*

'Hey, that one was all my own work!' Harry laughed.

Against Liverpool, Kieran chipped the ball cleverly over Dejan Lovren's head and Harry ran in and scored. *GOAL!*

Tottenham were flying but Kieran was about to face his toughest test yet – Real Madrid, the twelve-time Champions League winners. He would be taking on the most lethal left wing in the world: Marcelo and Cristiano Ronaldo.

'Come on, we can beat them!' Kieran shouted in the dressing room before kick-off. He was Tottenham's first-choice now, and he feared no-one.

As the two teams walked out at Wembley, Kieran was hit by a wall of deafening noise. There were over 83,000 fans in the stadium and almost all of them were cheering for Tottenham.

Come on you Spurs!

Kieran didn't look up, though. He kept his eyes fixed on the grass in front of him. He was fully focused on winning this massive football match.

'When Marcelo pushes up, he leaves a big gap behind him,' Pochettino had told Kieran. 'That's your space to run into!'

Midway through the first half, Harry Winks got the ball in central midfield and played a brilliant pass out to the right. Marcelo watched it fly over his head and then turned to find... Kieran! He was doing exactly what his manager had asked him to. Kieran watched the ball carefully onto his right foot and crossed it first-time to Dele. *GOAL!*

Tottenham were beating Real Madrid! Kieran

chased after Dele, pumping his fists at the cheering crowd.

For Kieran, 2017 really had turned out to be his year. Not only had he become Tottenham's first-choice and an England international, but now he had an assist against Real Madrid in the Champions League. It was his thirteenth in all competitions, six more than any other Premier League defender.

'That pass was world-class!' Dele told him.

As Kieran looked over at the bench, Pochettino gave him a big thumbs-up. Their plan had worked but now Spurs had some defending to do.

Kieran kept his eyes on the ball as Ronaldo dribbled into the penalty area. Real Madrid's superstar danced from side to side, with a stepover to the left, and then a stepover to the right, but he didn't make a silly tackle. When Ronaldo eventually decided to shoot, Kieran blocked it.

'Great work, Tripps!' Hugo shouted.

Kieran was having his best game ever. On the edge of the Real Madrid box, he showed off some stepovers of his own. He beat Isco and then nutmegged Marcelo.

Trippier! Trippier!

The Spurs fans loved him. In the second half, Kieran even made a goal line clearance to stop Ronaldo from scoring. Eventually, he did get a goal but it was too little too late. 3–1 – Tottenham had beaten Real Madrid!

'We did it!' Kieran cried out at the final whistle, hugging Dele.

The Spurs players walked around the Wembley pitch, clapping their amazing supporters. They were through to the next round of the Champions League!

Kieran was in dreamland but a few weeks later, there was a horrible wake-up call awaiting him. It was Manchester City vs Tottenham, Kyle vs Kieran.

After months playing as an attacking wing-back, Kieran returned to his old right-back role. It turned out to be a total disaster. City's winger Leroy Sané skipped past him again and again.

'I need some help here!' Kieran called out to his teammates.

He couldn't even get his crosses right. 'Sorry!' Kieran shouted as the ball sailed high over Dele's head. Tottenham were lucky to be losing only 1–0 at half-time, but it wasn't long until things got a whole lot worse.

City were running riot down the left. Kieran was way out of position as Kevin De Bruyne dribbled forward. He sprinted back as fast as he could but it was no use. 2–0 to City!

Ten minutes later, Sané escaped past Kieran and crossed to Raheem. 3–0!

'Offside!' Kieran cried out hopefully but the linesman's flag stayed down.

The match ended in a humiliating 4–1 defeat for Tottenham. It was a painful reminder for Kieran that he wasn't a superstar yet. In the dressing room afterwards, he didn't hide away. He owned up to his errors.

'I let everyone down today,' he told his manager and teammates, 'but it won't happen again, I promise.'

Kieran didn't let one bad game get him down. He soon went back to being Spurs' Mr Consistent on the right:

Tottenham 2–0 Manchester United,

and Tottenham 1–0 Arsenal!

'North London is white, not red!' Kieran cheered at

full-time.

Sadly, 2017–18 had turned out to be yet another trophy-free season for Spurs. They lost to Juventus in the Champions League Round of 16, to Manchester United in the FA Cup semi-final, and to Kyle's Manchester City in the Premier League title race.

'We can't keep getting so close,' Kieran moaned. 'Eventually, we've got to go all the way and win something!'

His strong season wasn't over yet, though. On 16 May 2018, Southgate announced his England squad for the World Cup in Russia. The FA released a video where each player's name was revealed one by one. Raheem was first, then John Stones, then Trent Alexander-Arnold. Eventually, the video zoomed in on a boy in Bury:

'KIERAN TRIPPIER!' he said. 'Go on, lad!'

Kieran, Harry, Dele, Danny and Eric – they were all off to Russia together!

After telling his proud parents, Kieran tweeted his followers: 'It's an honour to be named in the England squad. I can't wait for my first World Cup.'

CHAPTER 23

A WORLD CUP TO REMEMBER

It may have been Kieran's first World Cup, but would he actually get to play? Kyle was off to Russia too, so would Kieran just be England's back-up right-back?

No, because Southgate had found a brilliant way to fit them both into the same starting line-up. In the pre-tournament friendlies, the manager moved Kyle to the back three and brought Kieran in as the wing-back. Problem solved!

Netherlands 0–1 England,

England 1–1 Italy,

England 2–1 Nigeria.

'It's like the Under-19s all over again!' Kieran and Kyle joked.

It was so much fun that the two could play together again in the same team. They formed a perfect partnership down the England right. Kyle provided the speed and Kieran provided the crosses. Against Nigeria, he curled a corner-kick into the six-yard box for Gary Cahill to score. *GOAL!*

Kieran couldn't wait for the World Cup to get started. England had a great group of players and everyone got on really well with each other. At the base camp in Repino, he didn't just hang out with his Tottenham teammates; he hung out with everyone!

One day after training, Kieran played ten-pin bowling with Trent, Gary and Jesse Lingard. Another day, he played with Jack Butland and Jordan Henderson, who was dreadful.

'Maybe you should stick to football, Hendo!'

Ahead of the first match against Tunisia, Southgate sorted out England's set-piece tactics. He gave Kieran and Ashley Young the important task of taking all the corners and free kicks.

'It's a key part of our game-plan,' Southgate told them, 'so we're relying on you guys to get it right!'

'Yes, Boss!'

Kieran would take the corners from the right, and Ashley would take the corners from the left. But when it came to free kicks, they would have to battle it out amongst themselves. They spent hours playing 'first to twenty free kicks' after training. Their contests were a lot closer than the ones Kieran used to have with Steve at Manchester City.

'This one to win it, Youngie... Get in!'

England's game-plan worked straight away. In the tenth minute against Tunisia, Ashley's corner reached John Stones at the back post. The keeper saved his powerful header but Harry was in the right place at the right time for the rebound. 1–0!

'What a start!' Kieran cheered as he jumped on Harry. Soon, they were both at the bottom of a big team bundle.

England were on fire and they should have scored a second goal but instead, they conceded one. A cross came in from the left and Kyle fouled the Tunisia striker. Penalty!

'No way, ref!' Kyle and Kieran protested in unison

but it was no use. 1–1!

England had to stay strong and fight back. Kieran was their star player, creating chance after chance for his team. If he kept delivering incredible crosses, surely Harry or Dele would score eventually. It had worked so many times at Tottenham.

In the last minute of the match, England won a corner on the right. Kieran took a deep breath and aimed for the penalty spot. As usual, the cross was perfect. Harry Maguire won the first header and Harry Kane scored from the second. 2–1!

This time, Kieran was the last player to join the big team bundle because he had to run all the way across the pitch. It was worth it, though. He was an England World Cup hero now!

'I couldn't have done it without you, guys!' Harry Kane said at the final whistle, with one arm around Ashley, and the other around Kieran.

When he checked his phone, Kieran had so many messages.

'Congrats, Tripps, what a performance!' said Ben.

'Very proud of you, kid,' said Jim.

'Bro, you've created the most goalscoring chances in the World Cup so far!' said Kelvin.

It was a night that Kieran would never ever forget. He had come a very long way since that early loan spell at Barnsley.

And he was only just getting started. In the eighth minute against Panama, Kieran curled another corner-kick towards the penalty spot. This time, it was John who headed the ball home. 1–0!

'Come on!' Kieran shouted in front of the fans.

The match finished 6–1 to England. With two wins, they were through to the Round of 16. Back home, the nation began to believe:

It's coming home, it's coming home,
It's coming, FOOTBALL'S COMING HOME!'

The England players, however, were not getting carried away. It was knock-out football from now on. One mistake could really cost them, especially against a top team like Colombia.

'If we play our way, we can win this!' Southgate

assured them before kick-off.

Back at the 1998 World Cup, Beckham had scored that fantastic free kick against Colombia. Kieran remembered watching it on TV with his dad. Twenty years on, could he copy his childhood hero?

Hopefully!

Kieran was a man on a mission. He burst down the right wing and delivered the cross, but Harry Kane's header landed on top of the net.

'Great ball, Tripps!' he called out with a big thumbs-up. 'Keep them coming!'

Early in the second half, Kieran aimed for Harry again from a corner. The England captain ran towards the ball but he was being fouled. Penalty!

Harry wasn't going to miss from the spot. 1–0! As long as they defended well, England were heading into the World Cup quarter-finals.

'Keep your concentration!' Southgate urged.

But right at the end, Colombia's centre-back Yerry Mina won a header in the penalty area. Kieran was there on the goal line but he couldn't keep it out. 1–1!

'No, no, NO!' he screamed, staring down at his feet.

They couldn't give up now. England battled on through extra time to penalties. Uh-oh! They had lost so many shoot-outs in the past, but this time the team was well-prepared. They had practised for this and Southgate knew his top five takers:

Harry Kane... scored!

Marcus Rashford... scored!

Jordan Henderson... missed!

Oh no, were they going to lose on penalties yet again? Colombia missed their third spot-kick, which meant England had the chance to equalise. Kieran walked slowly forward, from the halfway line to the spot.

'Don't rush. Take your time!' his manager had told him.

Kieran didn't get to take penalties for Burnley or Tottenham but he used to take lots when he was younger and he never missed. If he could do it in the FA Youth Cup, then he could surely do it in the World Cup too.

With a deep breath, he ran forward and... scored! It was a perfect penalty, right in the top corner. The Colombian keeper had no chance. Kieran calmly turned to his teammates on the halfway line and pumped his fist.

'Nice one, Tripps!' Jesse yelled out.

Kieran's spot-kick had given his team the advantage. Jordan Pickford saved the next Colombian penalty and then Eric scored. It was over – England had won their first-ever World Cup shoot-out!

'We did it!' Kieran roared loud and proud as his country celebrated a famous victory.

'It's coming home, it's coming home,
It's coming, FOOTBALL'S COMING HOME!'

What a wonderful first World Cup it was turning out to be! In the space of two weeks, Kieran had gone from unsung wing-back to 'The Bury Beckham'. In the stadium in Moscow, Charlotte lifted up their young son, Jacob, so that he could get a better view of the action.

'Your daddy's a national hero now!'

Could England now go all the way and lift the trophy? Why not? With Kieran crossing the ball to Harry, they could beat anyone. They had a strong team spirit and 53 million people cheering them on.

With a 2–0 win over Sweden, the Three Lions were into the semi-finals. One more win, and Kieran would be playing in a World Cup final.

The last team standing in their way was Croatia. They had top-quality players like Luka Modrić and Mario Mandžukić, but if England could get off to another good start...

When Dele won an early free kick, Kieran got ready to shoot. 'I've got this, Youngie!' he told Ashley confidently. Then he ran up and curled the ball over the wall and into the top corner.

Goooooooooooooooooooooaaaaaaaaaaaaaaaaallllllllllll lllllllllllll!!!!!!!!!!!!!!!!!!!

What a start, and what a way to score your first-ever England goal! Kieran felt on top of the world as he slid across the grass on his knees.

That fantastic feeling lasted all the way until the

sixty-eighth minute. But after Croatia equalised, England's exhausted players were fighting a losing battle.

'Keep going!' Southgate shouted from the sidelines.

His team struggled on but eventually in extra-time, Mandžukić scored the winning goal for Croatia. England were left devastated and defeated. They had got so close to the World Cup final.

Unfortunately, Kieran couldn't carry on. He limped off the pitch with tears in his eyes, as the fans clapped and cheered. It wasn't how he wanted to end his life-changing tournament. But even so, he had arrived in Russia as an underrated right-back, and was now leaving as a national hero – just like all of the England players.

'Last night hurt and will for a while but we must take positives from the last few weeks and look forward to the future,' he posted on Twitter. 'It's been a journey that we can all be proud of.'

What a journey it had been for Kieran. Like the England team in Russia, he had overcome so many obstacles. From his back garden in Bury, he had battled through rejection at Manchester City and relegation at Burnley to make it all the way to the top. He was now first-choice at Tottenham and only the third England player ever to score in a World Cup semi-final. Even his hero Becks couldn't compete with that.

Turn the page for a sneak preview of another
brilliant football story by Matt and Tom
Oldfield. . .

PICKFORD

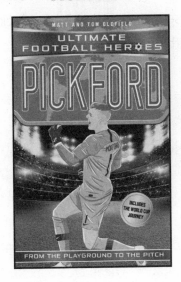

CHAPTER 1

ENGLAND'S PENALTY HERO

Otkritie Arena, Moscow, 3 July 2018

The tired England team assembled on the pitch. After 120 nail-biting minutes, only a penalty shoot-out stood between them and the World Cup quarter-finals. They needed a hero. Could it be their young keeper, playing in only his seventh international match? Jordan took a deep breath and believed.

Colombia's late equaliser had been a crushing blow. After making a super save to deny Mateus Uribe, Jordan just couldn't keep out Yerry Mina's powerful header.

'Now we'll just have to do it the hard way,' Jordan said to himself.

Still, Gareth Southgate looked like the calmest person in the stadium. 'Okay lads, we knew penalties were part of the deal in the knockout rounds,' he said. 'We're ready for this.'

Jordan nodded. They had spent hours practising on the training ground to make sure that they were all as comfortable as possible if it came to this.

He watched Gareth walk from player to player, checking on injuries and last-minute confidence levels.

'All good?' he asked Marcus and Kieran.

Both looked straight at their manager and nodded. No hesitation. While the physios worked quickly to heal players' tired legs, Gareth wrote down five names on a sheet of paper for the referee:

Harry Kane, Marcus Rashford, Jordan Henderson (or Hendo, as everyone called him), Kieran Trippier, Eric Dier.

'Remember everything we've talked about,' Harry shouted over the noise from the crowd. 'Pick your spot and be decisive. Don't feel rushed, and just ignore their keeper.'

'Come on, boys!' Jordan yelled, jumping up and down to release some of the nervous energy.

Jordan had his own plan to follow. After watching hundreds of clips of penalties on his laptop, he had sat down with England's other goalkeepers, Jack Butland and Nick Pope, to decide on the team tactics. Which way should he dive for each of Colombia's takers? He was leaving nothing to chance.

'Here you go,' Jack said, handing him a water bottle, which had notes written on it. 'Good luck!'

'Thanks, mate!' Jordan replied.

He gripped the bottle tightly as he read the words. He felt ready for the biggest moment of his life.

Harry was back from the coin toss. 'We're going second, lads,' he said.

Gareth had a few final words: 'I'm so proud of all of you. So are all the fans. This is just one more test laid out in front of us. Now go and be heroes!' The players all clapped and cheered.

As they walked over to the halfway line, Gareth put his arm around Jordan. 'There isn't any other shot-stopper in the world I'd want protecting our net tonight. Just trust your instincts.'

Jordan felt ten feet tall. He didn't know what to say so he just high-fived Gareth and then jogged over to the far end of the pitch. He was in his zone now, but he took a minute to glance at the England flags behind the goal. Even from a distance, he could see the passion. There was fear too. Penalties had not been kind to England in the past. In fact, they had never won a World Cup shoot-out. Ever!

'You can do this, Jordan!' the supporters shouted. He winked back at them. Yes, he could!

As he walked over to the goal, Jordan tucked his bottle into a red towel so that the Colombia keeper wouldn't spot England's secret plan. What if David Ospina asked to have a sip of water? That would be a disaster!

Luckily, he didn't. Jordan took one last look at his bottle and then stepped onto his line. Radamel Falcao was up first. Jordan waited as long as he could before diving to his right, but Falcao placed it perfectly down the middle. 1–0!

Jordan dragged himself up, shaking his head. 'Forget it and move on,' he told himself. There would be other chances to save the day.

He had a more important job to do first. He grabbed the ball and carried it over to Harry. This was part of Gareth's plan. It gave the Colombian keeper one fewer reason to approach the England penalty takers to put them off.

'You've got this, big man,' he said, patting Harry on the shoulder.

Harry smashed his penalty into the bottom corner. Unstoppable – 1–1!

Jordan guessed the right way on Colombia's second penalty, but Juan Cuadrado picked out the top corner. 2–1!

When Marcus' perfect strike made it 2–2, the pressure went up another level. On his way back to the halfway line, Marcus ran over to Jordan to bump fists. 'We believe in you, man,' he said, pointing at his goalkeeper as he walked away. 'A big save is coming. I know it!'

Colombia made no mistake with their third

penalty either. Jordan tried not to panic. He
was getting a good spring off his line, but the
Colombians had not given him a sniff so far. Still,
he could see that they had put all their best
penalty takers first.

Seconds later, his heart sank. Hendo hit his penalty
well but the Colombian keeper guessed right and
pushed it out... *Saved!*

Now Jordan really had to step up, or England's
World Cup dream would be over.

He went through the same routine again:
bouncing on his line, making himself big, timing his
dive. He correctly guessed left for the fourth penalty
but saw the ball fly high above his dive. He turned to
see it crash off the bar and bounce safely away from
the goal... *Miss!*

'Yeeeeeeees!' he screamed, looking over at his
teammates. The England fans roared. They were
back in it.

Kieran kept his nerve with a beautiful penalty.
3–3! It was basically sudden death now.

Jordan tried to stay calm but his heart was racing

after the Colombia miss. He felt even more confident now.

'One stop, one stop,' he mumbled under his breath. That might be all it took to become England's penalty hero.

As Carlos Bacca stepped up for Colombia's fifth penalty, the crowd fell silent. Jordan watched Bacca run up and then he sprung to his right. His eyes lit up as the ball curled towards him. But he was diving too far. Almost in slow motion, he threw up his left hand desperately. The ball was well hit but his hand stayed strong, clawing the penalty away... *Saved!*

'Come oooooooooooooon!'

Jordan leapt to his feet and punched the air again and again, screaming as loud as he could. The plan had worked. He had just saved a penalty in a World Cup shoot-out! Now England were one kick away from the quarter-finals.

He looked towards the halfway line and saw the huge smiles on his teammates' faces. They stood with their arms linked, ready to sprint forward if everything went to plan.

Jordan felt like he was shaking as he passed the ball to Eric, but he tried not to show it. 'Just take your time,' he said.

Eric did just that. He paced out his run-up, waited for the whistle and then swept the ball low into the bottom corner. England had done it!

The next few minutes were a blur. Jordan leapt in the air and turned to run towards the halfway line. But he was too late. His teammates were already racing over to *him*, England's penalty hero. Harry and Kieran jumped on his back. Then John Stones and Marcus, followed by the whole team.

'You legend!' Kieran screamed.

'I owe you big time!' Hendo called, ruffling Jordan's hair.

Jordan savoured every second with his teammates, who had become his friends over the past few weeks. They hugged and laughed as it all began to sink in. Happiness, relief and exhaustion – all the emotions mixed together.

Gareth joined in the celebrations, hugging every player and saving the biggest one for Jordan. 'I told you!' he laughed, jabbing Jordan playfully in the ribs. 'I knew you'd do something special tonight.'

Then they ran over to the fans – or limped over, in most cases. Tomorrow, they would be sore, but tonight they were buzzing too much to feel it. The England players had given their nation something to really cheer about.

'They've had to wait a long time for this!' Jordan shouted to Harry.

'Get right at the front, Jordan. You're the hero tonight!' Harry nudged him forward, so that the fans could sing his name:

Rhythm is a dancer,
Pickford is the answer,
Saving shots from everywhere!

Jordan couldn't believe what he was hearing. What a feeling! The players took photo after photo before finally reaching the section where their families stood waiting. He spotted his girlfriend, Megan, in the crowd and blew her a kiss. It meant so much that she was in the stadium to see it all. He could only imagine the celebrations back in England. He remembered that a lot of his friends had been planning to watch the game together, and that made him even prouder.

Jordan could feel happy tears building up and the hairs on the back of his neck stood on end. He just didn't want the night to end. The England fans were in no hurry to go home either.

When the players finally got back to the dressing room, Gareth called for quiet.

'Lads, take a moment to think about what you've just achieved. I could not be prouder of every single one of you. That took guts. We had to fight for everything. They kicked us all over the pitch, but we kept our cool and never gave up.

'And those were terrific penalties, including yours Hendo. I will remember this moment for a very long time. Let's enjoy it tonight. You deserve that. But we've got more memories to make, starting with either Sweden or Switzerland on Saturday. This is just the beginning for this team!'

The players did not have the energy to stand up, but they clapped and cheered. Jordan was so happy for his manager, who had famously dealt with penalty shoot-out heartbreak as an England player, back at Euro 96.

There was only one song for the players to sing. Eric turned on the music and cranked up the volume:

*'It's coming home, it's coming home,
It's coming, FOOTBALL'S COMING HOME!'*

'If you'd told me five years ago that I'd be saving a penalty at the 2018 World Cup, I'd have laughed in your face,' Jordan told Kieran, giggling. 'I was playing in League Two! It's been such a crazy journey, but it's all worth it now. It doesn't get any better than this!'

As he took off his socks and grabbed a towel, Jordan thought about his journey again – the highs, the lows, the doubts. He was still only twenty-four, but it had been quite a ride so far!

Manchester City Youth

🏆 FA Youth Cup: 2007–08

Burnley

🏆 Football League Championship runner-up:
2013–14

Individual

🏆 Barnsley Young Player of the Year: 2010–11
🏆 Burnley Player of the Year: 2011–12
🏆 PFA Championship Team of the Year: 2012–13,
2013–14

TRIPPIER

2 & 12

THE FACTS

NAME: KIERAN JOHN TRIPPIER

DATE OF BIRTH: 19 September 1990

AGE: 24

PLACE OF BIRTH: Bury

NATIONALITY: English

BEST FRIEND: Ben Mee

CURRENT CLUB: Tottenham

POSITION: RB/RWB

THE STATS

Height (cm):	178
Club appearances:	309
Club goals:	11
Club trophies:	0
International appearances:	13
International goals:	1
International trophies:	0
Ballon d'Ors:	0

★ ★ ★ **HERO RATING: 82** ★ ★ ★

GREATEST MOMENTS

Type and search the web links to see the magic for yourself!

16 APRIL 2008,
MANCHESTER CITY 3-1 CHELSEA

https://www.youtube.com/watch?v=JNjcoTbGvBs

In the 2008 FA Youth Cup final, it was City's local lads against Chelsea's international squad of superstars. Even without Daniel Sturridge, City still managed to win! Vladimír Weiss was their free-kick king this time, but Kieran was as solid as ever at right-back. Sadly, he got injured in the last few minutes and missed the trophy celebrations.

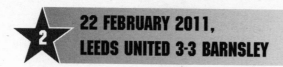

22 FEBRUARY 2011,
LEEDS UNITED 3-3 BARNSLEY

https://www.youtube.com/watch?v=1fO8Zapkmds

During his loan spell at Barnsley, Kieran quickly became the team's set-piece specialist. This free-kick against Leeds wasn't one of his best, but it was his first goal for the club and an important one too. Barnsley were losing the big Yorkshire Derby until Kieran rescued them with his remarkable right foot.

21 APRIL 2014,
BURNLEY 2-0 WIGAN ATHLETIC

https://www.youtube.com/watch?v=lEPUgaVslHg

This was the day when Kieran and Burnley achieved their dream of returning to the Premier League. At the final whistle, the jubilant fans stormed the pitch to celebrate with the players. Two years after leaving Manchester City behind, Kieran was back in the big-time with Burnley.

4 1 NOVEMBER 2017, TOTTENHAM 3-1 REAL MADRID

https://www.youtube.com/watch?v=VBVAGbm1wBs

Football games don't get much bigger than this – Real Madrid in the Champions League! But Kieran was totally fearless and gave one of the best performances of his life. Not only did he keep Cristiano Ronaldo and Marcelo quiet, but he also set up Spurs' first goal for Dele Alli with an incredible cross. At Wembley, Kieran proved that he was ready to play at the highest level.

5 11 JULY 2018, CROATIA 2-1 ENGLAND

https://www.youtube.com/watch?v=RbmaLT320hw

The 2018 World Cup semi-final ended in disappointment for England, but it was still an amazing moment when he scored his first-ever international goal with a fantastic free-kick that flew straight into the top corner. What a perfect way for 'The Bury Beckham' to complete his wonderful World Cup!

PLAY LIKE YOUR HEROES

'CROSS IT LIKE KIERAN'

SEE IT HERE You Tube

https://www.youtube.com/watch?v=QFFseyCoiCE

STEP 1: Keep making runs down the right wing until you receive that perfect pass…

Step 2: Look up. If your attackers are already on the move, then cross the ball early, maybe even first-time if you can.

Step 3: If they're not, take a touch to control the pass and wait until the time is right.

Step 4: BANG! Apply the right power to your cross. Who's your target, and how far away are they?

Step 5: If you're not aiming for a particular player, you want the ball to drop down in the danger zone between the penalty spot and the six-yard line.

Step 6: Put lots of curl on your cross, so that it's even more difficult for the defenders to deal with.

Step 7: GOAL! Make sure that you run over and celebrate. If it wasn't for your killer cross, there would be no goal!

TEST YOUR KNOWLEDGE

1. Who were Kieran's two big Manchester United heroes?

2. How did Kieran annoy the groundsman at the Manchester City academy?

3. Which club did Kieran's brother, Kelvin, play for?

4. Which club did Kieran's Manchester City team beat in the 2008 FA Youth Cup final?

5. Which country did Kieran's England Under-19s lose to in the 2009 European Championship final?

6. Which club was Kieran playing for when he got his first England Under-21 call-up?

7. Which Burnley manager led them to Premier League promotion in 2014?

8. How many games did Kieran miss during the 2014–15 Premier League season?

9. How much money did Tottenham pay to sign Kieran from Burnley?

10. Who was Kieran's big right-back rival for Tottenham and England?

11. How many goals did Kieran score at the 2018 World Cup?

Answers below. . . No cheating!

1. David Beckham and Gary Neville 2. By kicking balls at him and then hiding! 3. Oldham Athletic 4. Chelsea 5. Ukraine 6. Barnsley 7. Sean Dyche 8. Zero! 9. £3.5million 10. Kyle Walker 11. Trick question! The answer is two, if you include his penalty in the shoot-out against Colombia.

The 2018 World Cup saw England's young lions produce their best performance for a generation, and storm to the semi-finals of the World Cup.

Complete your collection with these international edition Ultimate Football Heroes.

AVAILABLE NOW